CARING *for our* COMMUNITY

The History of Mid Coast Hospital

To Bridget
With best wishes,
Herb Paris
Nov. 2015

HERBERT PARIS

THIS BOOK

IS DEDICATED TO

The Staff and Volunteers

OF *Mid Coast Health Services.*

SURGIT NEC MERGITUR
(Whatever the storm the ship sails on, it never sinks.)

The more I came to realize the important personal nature of a high quality community hospital and the culture of "neighbors caring for neighbors," I became convinced the hospital that I had come to steward could grow, develop and represent excellence.

My vision encompassed a health care system that had significant community outreach, that could recruit outstanding staff and establish a system providing a continuum of care: from acute hospitalization to long term care; from rehabilitation services to home care; to hospice care; and from primary care and specialty care to referral affiliations for care that was beyond our capacity. Through my 33 year career in Brunswick, ME, together with an outstanding staff of colleagues and a supportive board of trustees that shared my vision, we made it all happen.

Upon my retirement it seemed appropriate and important to record the history and development of Bath Memorial Hospital, Regional Memorial Hospital and finally, Mid Coast Hospital and Mid Coast Health Services.

—Herbert Paris
2014

PREFACE

THE HISTORY of Mid Coast Hospital begins with Bath City Hospital in Bath, ME, and Regional Memorial Hospital in Brunswick, ME representing a period beginning in 1907 and continuing today as Mid Coast Hospital. The two hospitals had very different origins.

The Bath hospital represented the visionary thinking of the community leaders in 1907, who realized that the development of a hospital in Bath was an important step in the infrastructure and the future growth of the community. The hospital structure in Brunswick represented the more typical development of the cottage hospitals in this country, which were the antecedent to what is now known as the community hospital. Cottage hospitals were typically located in converted old mansions and owned and operated by physicians. It wasn't until the 1950s that the leadership of a cottage hospital in Brunswick recognized that such an institution was not sustainable into the future, and thus began the development of what was to become Regional Memorial Hospital. This story tells the history of these two hospitals and their successor, Mid Coast Hospital.

With my arrival as the administrator of Regional in 1978, the beginning of the pathway began which ultimately led to the consolidation, merger, and building of the healthcare system. My vision—that we had the capacity to build a continuum of care—was focused on meeting the needs of the greater Bath, Brunswick, Topsham and surrounding communities.

I had the unique opportunity during a 33 year period of being the president and chief executive officer to guide this vision and watch it materialize. Midcoast Hospital had a strong board of directors led by Richard A. Morrell, chairman, and an able and experienced management team. The system ultimately encompassed a flagship hospital providing acute care services to the community coupled with a broad outreach of health education, a range of health care services and preventive care programs. The system, as it was built, included long-term care, a multi-specialty group medical practice, assisted living units encompassing dementia care, an independent living retirement community, home health services and a hospice program.

Mid Coast Hospital currently occupies a cluster of modern buildings with 92 beds, extensive outpatient services and the latest in sophisticated medical technology in patient care. The hospital is recognized as a leader having earned MAGNET status from the American Nurse Credentialing Center of the American Nurses Association, meeting full requirements of the Joint Commission on Accreditation of Hospital Organizations, as well as state and federal accreditation agencies. Mid Coast enjoys the reputation of providing high quality care to the population it serves.

Aerial view Mid Coast Hospital circa 2012.

AKNOWLEDGEMENTS

IN PREPARING THIS BOOK I had the privilege of interviewing many people for information, assistance and guidance. When researching the records of Mid Coast Hospital, I had available a complete original set of the Board of Trustee minutes of the Bath hospital from 1907 as well as a complete set and founding documents and Board of Trustee minutes for Regional hospital beginning in 1957. I want to thank the Pejepscot Historical Society, the Bath Historical Society, the Maine Maritime Museum library, the Patten Free Library Sagadahoc History and Genealogy Room, the Curtis Library and the Bowdoin College Library for generously providing access to their collections.

I want to thank a number of people who had been associated with the hospitals for extended periods of time or whose roots stretch into the history of the development of the Bath and Regional hospitals. Old files and newspaper clippings, carefully bound in scrapbooks, were shared with me by employees who found these items in the basements and attics of their parents and grandparents' homes. I have attempted to detail as impartially as possible the consolidation and merger of the two hospitals during a period in which there was great community concern about the loss of their community hospitals.

This book explains certain sensitive topics and controversies in the hospitals' history including those that occurred in the relatively recent past.

BIW

Although it would have been easy for me to skip over these controversies and avoid unpleasant details, it would have resulted in a dishonest and incomplete story. It would also have been easy for me to disagree or to sit in judgment of certain practices or individuals. But I did not feel that this would be an appropriate role to play. Nor did I think that it would enhance the book's value.

Interviews with participants in the Mid Coast history as well as with key observers constituted a major and invaluable primary source of information. These interviews were conducted over a period of several years and sadly some people I interviewed have since passed away.

Researching and writing this book has been a pleasure because I have been part of the history for 33 years. Personal recollection explains the paucity of footnotes and references in the last one third of the time covered in this book.

I want to especially acknowledge the help and support that I received from my colleagues, Marla Davis, RN, a long-time employee of Mid Coast Hospital and director of our Community Health and Wellness Programs, and G. Baer Connard, Jr., a former resident of Bath whose family played an important role in the leadership of the Bath hospital during the 1940s and 1950s. Their research and contributions to this effort were invaluable and the three of us served as the editorial board. I also want to acknowledge the graciousness of Julia Wilson Stevens of Harpswell, whose father Dr. Clement Wilson, owned Dr. Wilson's hospital in Brunswick; and to Miss Margaret Dunlop and Miss Helen Johnson for their time and willingness to participate in an interview in which we discussed Miss Dunlop's remembrances of Dr. C. Earle Richardson's hospital in Brunswick. Her mother served as Director of Nursing there for 20 years. Miss

An aerial view of Bath and the Kennebec River from the North, prior to the construction of the Sagadahoc Bridge.

TOM JONES

An aerial view of downtown Brunswick from the West, with the Cabot Mill (Fort Andross) and the Androscoggin River in the foreground.

Johnson's father, Dr. Henry Johnson, practiced medicine in Brunswick at the same time as he served as the Bowdoin College physician. I gained insight into Regional from Gayle Hayes, RN, a former head nurse of the operating room, and Dr. James Fife, a respected surgeon who practiced in Brunswick from 1962 until 1994. I appreciated William Haggett sharing his thoughts and insights as chairman of the Commission on Hospital Costs. Anne Marsh, retired executive director of the Pine Tree Society in Bath, provided information on the Hyde Memorial Home for Crippled Children. Also, I wish to acknowledge, with great appreciation, Cheryl Roney, who painstakingly translated my dictation onto the printed page and has helped immeasurably in getting this story into its final form.

A special note of thanks and recognition to Marc Voyvodich who served as the Mid Coast Health Services planning consultant during the post consolidation period when planning was vital to what the total program of Mid Coast Health Services would look like in the future.

I want to thank Lauren Doran, Robert McCue, Barbara McCue, Harriet Paris, David Paris and Millie Stewart who read the draft of this book and made valuable suggestions, corrections and editorial criticisms. I want to acknowledge with appreciation the many helpful suggestions made by Michael Mahan of Mahan Graphics of Bath during the preparation of this manuscript.

I appreciated the help of Michael Doucette of Just Framing in Bath, Gerry Maraghy of Mid Coast Hospital and Jeff Morris of Pierce Studio, Brunswick in preparing the images used in this book. Finally, I want to thank Robert McCue and Lois Skillings for contributing the epilogue covering the period from my retirement to the publication of this book.

INTRODUCTION

THE CITY OF BATH and the Town of Brunswick lie in the Southern mid coast region of Maine, 10 miles apart. The two communities are connected by a slice of the Route One corridor, which, before the construction of I-95, served as the major route from the Canadian border to the Florida Keys.

Based upon 2010 census data, the population of Brunswick stands at 20,278, and the population of Bath at 8,514. As centers for commerce and services, the Bath and Brunswick communities are a hub for more than 12 other small communities on their periphery, for a combined population of nearly 80,000.

The demographics of this population indicate a community with a balanced distribution of young and old, and one which is relatively well-off financially as compared to other Maine communities. Nearly three-quarters of all the housing units in the area are occupied by their owners. The average size of families in the region is just over three people. Family incomes average in the mid 30,000 dollars, well above most Maine communities. Over 20% of its population is 16 years or younger, and slightly over 12% of the population is 65 years or older. The racial make up of the two communities is predominately Caucasian; the religion is mostly Protestant.

Despite their adjacency, Bath and Brunswick share a history more characterized by competition than collaboration. A classic rivalry of high school sports is firmly entrenched. The self-perception of Bath as a hard-working, blue collar shipbuilding town stands in contrast to Brunswick's self-perception of a genteel college community.

A more complete understanding of the differences and commonalties of the two communities require a brief look at their historical roots.

A THUMBNAIL HISTORY OF BRUNSWICK

Brunswick evolved from a land grant on the Kennebec River bestowed by the Plymouth colony in 1629 to settlers who, it was thought, would help to pay off Plymouth's debt to English investors by fur trade with the Indians. Brunswick's location, at the confluence of the Androscoggin River, the Kennebec River, and Casco Bay, made it a perfect site for the first area sawmill, built in 1717.

In 1735, a petition signed by 29 citizens was presented to the legislature governing the district of Massachusetts, now called Maine, forming the town of Brunswick. Incorporated in the year 1739, Brunswick was the 11th town in the Province of Maine, and the most easterly of Cumberland County. Originally a collection of farms and outlying houses, Brunswick had started to develop the rudiments of a unified township by 1750.

Beginning about 1753, the first of many dams was built, and industry began to flourish along the river banks. In 1809, the first cotton mill was

Stowe House

BOWDOIN COLLEGE

built, a foothold for what was to become the town's dominant industry for over 100 years. In addition to cotton, wood paper pulp, paper boxes and lumber, carpentry and pumps, soap, marble and granite work, carriages and harnesses, leather, furniture, boots and shoes, washing machines, meal and flour, confectionery, ships and boats were manufactured in Brunswick.

The beginning of its development as an urban center must acknowledge Bowdoin College, established in 1794. This distinguished center of learning was named for James Bowdoin, former governor of Massachusetts when Maine was still a part of Massachusetts. Reverend Joseph McKeen was the first president. Among its early graduates were Nathaniel Hawthorne, Henry Wadsworth Longfellow, Admiral Robert Peary and General Joshua Chamberlain. As a result of the Missouri Compromise in 1820, Maine became a state in order to balance politically the slave states and the free states. Maine adopted the motto *Dirigo* meaning "I lead."

Brunswick was a way station in the Underground Railroad. The Underground Railroad was an informal network of persons who, although in violation of the "Fugitive Slave Act," helped escaped slaves reach freedom in Northern States and Canada. The Underground Railroad wasn't a railroad nor was it underground. It was actually a system where slaves would go from safehouse to safehouse until they could escape to freedom. Brunswick's most influential contribution to the abolitionist movement was Harriet Beecher Stowe, the wife of Brunswick minister, Calvin Ellis Stowe. She was inspired during a service at the First Parish Church to write *Uncle Tom's Cabin*, which was published in 1851.

Brunswick's economy gradually evolved to one based on manufacturing rather than on agrarian activities such as farming, fishing, and logging. Brunswick was second only to Bath in u.s. ship production between 1789 and 1807. In the southernmost part of town are several protected havens where ships were built, especially Pennellville.

Rail lines to Brunswick first opened in 1849, greatly enhancing the town's growth. An influx of Irish immigrant rail workers comprised a growing segment of the population. Brunswick became a major rail junction, and served as the hub for trains bound for Lewiston, Rockland, and Augusta.

Similar to every other New England mill town, Brunswick had a large population of French Canadian immigrants who worked at the textile mill. They brought with them social, cultural, and religious ways of life still evident today. The French immigration from Canada ceased altogether during the Depression of the 1930s.

A plant to produce gas to light the mill was built in 1859, and was also the original source of gas and electricity for the town. Gas street lights

An early view of Maine Street, Brunswick.

were installed in the downtown area about 1864; an electric generating plant was built near the mill dam in 1887.

In response to the diphtheria epidemic of 1886, the state ordered the mill owners to provide inoculations to their employees. Several unsatisfactory alternatives were tested to provide an unpolluted and constant supply of water, ending in the successful formation of the Brunswick and Topsham Water District in 1903.

Brunswick began to change most profoundly at the onset of World War II. The population grew rapidly after Brunswick was chosen as the site for the United States Naval Air Station. After the war, the base was decommissioned and absorbed by Bowdoin College and the University of Maine, only to be recommissioned in the late 1940s, and then decommissioned again in 2011. Intensified wartime activity at the Bath Iron Works (BIW) had its impact upon neighboring Brunswick as well. BIW bought land for a steel fabrication plant in East Brunswick, at the Harding Station, and operated three shifts to keep up with the demand. The influx of workers necessitated new housing developments and associated services to support them. The population of Brunswick grew by about 50% during the war.

A THUMBNAIL HISTORY OF BATH

The City of Bath has been most profoundly shaped by its heritage of shipbuilding which began in 1607 with the construction of *The Virginia*, the first seagoing vessel built in North America. Once considered the greatest shipbuilding port in the world, Bath is still home of the Bath Iron Works, one of the largest private employer in the state of Maine.

Bath was the first permanent settlement on the Kennebec River. Located 10 miles northeast of Brunswick, its location is 12 miles from the mouth of the Kennebec River, an area ideal for shipbuilding due to the unique topography. In fact, around the time of its settlement in 1660, the area was originally named "Long Reach," after this three mile long, half mile wide section of the river which provided good launching conditions.

Bath was the point of origin for many distinguished classes of vessels, including full-rigged ships, barques, schooners, speedy half-clippers, the *Ranger*, an America's Cup defender in 1938, and many types of gunboats, cruisers, and destroyers built for the United States Navy. During Bath's peak of wooden ship building, in the late 1800s, about 20 shipyards ran along the shores of the Long Reach.

There was a decline in Bath's economy during the post Civil War period. This was a time of transition from sailing ships to steam and then to turbine powered ships. The founding of Hyde Windlass Co. in 1865, which

would become Bath Iron Works in 1884, helped to reverse the decline. Today, BIW remains one of the premier shipyards in the United States.

Bath continues to be a repository of ship and shipping lore. The downtown is filled with distinguished buildings from the days when shipping agents resided on the banks of the Kennebec, and sailors brought home exotic items from foreign ports.

Bath's topographical suitability for shipbuilding also left it susceptible to other woes. The high banks that parallel the river make development difficult, and historically have limited the city's growth. During the boom years of World War I temporary tent communities housed workers to fill round-the-clock schedules. It was a prelude to the 1929 Depression, which had an early start in Bath. Overruns in production were to depress merchant

1878 detail from a bird's eye view of Bath showing the town center and ship building wharfs. Published by JJ Stoner of Wisconsin.

shipbuilding for the next few years until the outbreak of World War II.

During World War II, BIW enjoyed the defense boom, which brought with it a huge population influx to the area. However, the picture once again changed during the 1950s and 1960s. When the U.S. Defense Department set up a competitive bidding system, BIW did not fare well. As a result, the company diversified into commercial shipbuilding, and it was not until the late 1970s that BIW would again be in a competitive and profitable position. Due to a successful mix of both private and naval contracts, BIW employed its greatest workforce in the early 1980s when over 10,000 people were employed at the shipyard. In the 1980s and 1990s, BIW went through a series of ownership changes resulting in its current ownership by the General Dynamics Corporation.

Bath Iron Works circa 1974

BIW

CARING FOR OUR COMMUNITIES

2

The EARLY DAYS *of* HEALTHCARE

THE EARLIEST EVIDENCE of a practitioner of the art of medicine and healing is in 1760 with Dr. Mrs. Samuel Lombard, also known as Grannie Lombard (1729–1817). She and her husband Samuel built a house on the Berry's Mill Road in West Bath. Her practice included caring for all the sick people and midwifery. According to stories handed down, she was always at the ready for a messenger to come by to get her. She crossed the road from her home to where there was a ledge from which she could mount the messenger's horse. Her practice provided care from Merrymeeting Bay to Phippsburg. She was, however, upstaged in history by her husband, who was among a group of West Bath farmers captured by the Indians in 1751 and taken north. He escaped on ice skates and made it back down the St. Lawrence and Kennebec Rivers to West Bath. (1)

Little is known of local healers in Brunswick and Harpswell other than the names of Hanna Stover and Judith Havard. The first record of small pox outbreak was in 1792 when a hospital was set up on the commons. (2)

Public health and maritime health have been joined since America's earliest history. Colonial Americans recognized that diseases arrived on their shores by way of sailors on foreign ships. In response to a severe outbreak of yellow fever, President John Adams signed the first Federal health law, "An Act for the Relief of Sick and Disabled Seamen," in 1798. Through this act grew the Marine Hospital Service and the birth of American hospitals.

Marine hospitals quickly developed at major seaports along the Atlantic coast. Administration of the hospitals became the responsibility of the U.S. Treasury Department which collected customs based on a small percentage of each sailors' wages to pay for the hospital service. This is essentially the first federal prepaid health plan.

A marine hospital was established in Bath at the southern end of Washington Street, where the Plant Memorial Home, built in 1917, is today. This riverside plot is still referred to as Hospital Point. Sources disagree on the exact timing of this startup; credible local historians of the period give both 1792 and 1820 as dates. Parker Reed (1895) described the hospital as "2 stories and square." Henry Wilson Owen (1936) listed 1820 for the establishment and Benjamin Bartlett, MD, as the first Medical Director.

Ships traveling from the West Indies to Bath carrying lumber to supply the shipbuilding industry were quarantined at Hospital Point in order to examine the sailors for any signs of plague or fever. The facility also provided certain routine care. Once a ship was cleared it went on its way to the Port of Bath to deliver its cargo. The Marine Hospital service continued until 1909. Sailors who needed direct care were transferred to the Martin's Point Marine Hospital in Portland. (2) (3)

HYDE MEMORIAL HOME FOR CRIPPLED CHILDREN

Bath became Maine's center of care for children and adults with crippling diseases when, in 1947, the mansion of ship builder John Sedgewick Hyde, known as Elmhurst, was gifted by the family to the Pine Tree Society for Crippled Children. In addition to 17 rooms, the mansion included an indoor swimming pool, solarium, greenhouse and ballroom.

The goals of the Society, then a member of the National Easter Seal Society, was to provide special teachers for handicapped children, transport them to hospitals and clinics, and to provide them with orthopedic appliances and services to aid their recovery. The Home was considered a

The John Hyde Estate building was donated to the Pine Tree Society in 1947. A 51-bed inpatient home was established for the rehabilitation of young polio victims. It closed in 1965.

PINE TREE SOCIETY

perfect match to the Society's mission, and Executive Director Marie Preston helped push a bill through the Maine legislature to appropriate funding for the children's education. Mrs. Preston also raised the significant funds to convert the mansion to a rehabilitation facility with 51 beds.

Little could Mrs. Preston, the Hyde family, or the Pine Tree Board of Directors have known how important this generous gift would be. Over 70 children were treated in the first year. In 1949, Maine's poliomyelitis epidemic forced the inpatient capacity to more than twice the intended caseload. During this epidemic, over 42,000 children contracted the disease country-wide. The children and young adults came to the Hyde Home on a three month trial basis, but most stayed up to six months.

The staff consisted of nurses, aides, physical and occupational therapists, and many volunteers. Dr. Francis Winchenbach, a long time Bath practitioner, was Medical Director. Treatment consisted of hot packs, exercises, gait training, crutches, braces, and pool therapy. Many local civic organizations supported the efforts by making quilts and providing holiday and birthday gifts, and baking treats for the children.

Dr. Salk's polio vaccine, developed in 1955, over time reduced the need for these services. The Hyde Memorial Home for Crippled Children was closed in 1965. The program was moved to the Maine Medical Center to be closer to higher density population. The Hyde School purchased the estate and began the residential high school there.

Above: *Young polio patients with two of their Hyde Home staff outside the Estate's main building. Staff member at left is Lois Burns.*

Below: *Hyde Home students in the classroom*

JACQUELINE MCMANN SYLVESTER PHOTOGRAPHY COLLECTION, BATH HISTORICAL SOCIETY, BATH, MAINE

Students of the Medical School of Maine.

MEDICAL EDUCATION AT BOWDOIN COLLEGE

A medical school was established in Brunswick in 1820. With the encouragement of the President of Bowdoin College and the enthusiasm of Dr. Nathan Smith—founder of the Dartmouth Medical School and a professor of medicine at Yale University—there was an enthusiastic response to building a medical school in the newly established State of Maine. When this proposal was embraced by the State Legislature, the notion of a new medical school was realized.

On June 27, 1820, the first Legislature of Maine established the Medical School of Maine, to be under the control of the trustees and overseers of Bowdoin College. With this action, the legislature granted $1,500 for procuring the necessary books and equipment and authorized an annual payment of $1,000 for general expenses. Temporary quarters were established in Massachusetts Hall.

The building came to be known as *the Medical College* and incorrectly suggested a separation of the Medical College from the rest of the activities of Bowdoin. There was, however, a subtle change in the relationship of the college and the commonwealth following the initial action of the legislature. It was believed that the state would continue to support the institution but this was abandoned at an early stage. Subsequent legislatures did not maintain this commitment.

It was easy to gain admission to the medical school and many candidates did so without benefit of any undergraduate training. Many students came to the medical school and stayed only a few months before finding a physician in practice with whom to apprentice. Between 1820 and 1860 the Medical School of Maine curriculum was based solely on lectures and demonstrations. Early in the 1840s the Maine legislature enacted a statute which allowed deceased individuals whose bodies were not claimed for burial by the family or next of kin to be used by the medical school for anatomical purposes. The medical school was required to pay the sum of $100 and to provide for a decent burial once the bodies were no longer needed for anatomical purposes. Clinical teaching only became part of the curriculum after the Civil War.

A most important event in the history of the medical school came in 1860-1861 when Adams Hall, a building especially adopted for use as the medical school was built. The inconvenience suffered in the cramped

Adams Hall was home to the Medical School of Maine until 1921, when it was closed by the College.

quarters of the Massachusetts Hall, the original location, had begun to seriously impact the prosperity of the medical school. Efforts to petition the legislature to aid in erecting a home for the medical school failed. Adams Hall was constructed through private donations that the college was successful in receiving. An interesting postscript is that Dr. Augustus Stinchfield, who graduated from the medical school in 1868, formed the original partnership with Dr. William Worrell Mayo that gave rise to the Mayo Clinic. (5) In 1897 Professor Charles S. Hutchins, a Bowdoin College physicist and scientist, was the maker of the first X-ray photograph ever made in the United States. (6)

The desirability of connecting the medical school to a teaching hospital became abundantly clear. Attempts to develop such a hospital in Brunswick were unsuccessful. Efforts were resumed in discussions with Maine General Hospital to move the medical school to Portland. The charter of Maine General Hospital specified the promotion of medical education as one of its purposes. It was planned that the last two years of the course of clinical education would be given in Portland. The college catalog of 1897 announcing the Medical School of Maine would relocate to Portland, but the plan never came to pass with a final rejection from Maine General Hospital. There is some evidence to suggest that the lack of a progressive spirit among the hospital Board of Directors, its staff and superintendent, was a principal factor that propelled this rejection. (7) In the last report of 1898, President William DeWitt Hyde of Bowdoin stated the arguments for remaining in Brunswick and indicated that Bowdoin would build a cottage hospital in Brunswick. (8) Instead Maine General Hospital in

1900 assumed responsibility of providing clinical instruction to Bowdoin students. This collaboration provided the students with a high level of practical experience and guaranteed that graduating doctors would be well acquainted with Maine General as a place to practice their calling.

The Medical School of Maine subsequently acquired a building located at 72 Federal St. in Brunswick for the purpose of developing a cottage hospital on the site. However, there is no history that the facility ever became a clinical site for the care of patients in the Brunswick community and there is no indication that it ever functioned as a hospital.

In 1904 the American Medical Association (AMA) established a council on medical education, with a mandate to elevate and standardize the requirements for medical education. As one of the first acts, the council formulated a minimum standard for physician education calling for four years of high school, and an equal period of medical training and passage of a licensing test. Its ideal standard stipulated five years of medical school including one year of basic sciences, later folded into the pre-medical curriculum in colleges and an additional year of hospital internship. In an effort to identify and pressure weaker institutions, the AMA council began grading medical schools according to the record of their graduates on state licensing examinations Later it extended the evaluation to include the curriculum, facilities, faculty, and requirements for admission. In 1906 the AMA inspected the 160 schools then in existence and fully approved only 82, which it rated Class A. Class B consisted of 46 imperfect but redeemable institutions while 32 were rated beyond salvage fell into Class C.

In 1910, the Flexner Report, authored by a young Johns Hopkins University educator Abraham Flexner, was commissioned by the American Medical Association and funded by the Carnegie Foundation to review the standards and qualities of medical school teaching in the United States. This report gave an unfavorable review of the Medical School of Maine. In New England only Harvard and Yale escaped Flexner's censure. He suggested that the Medical School of Maine, along with the medical schools of Dartmouth, Vermont, Tufts and Boston University, as well as many others, simply were not worth saving.

Of the Medical School of Maine, Flexner wrote:

> *The laboratory branches are taught in the medical school building at Brunswick with the exception of chemistry, which is well provided for in the college laboratories; the equipment covering physiology, bacteriology, and pathology is slender. There is nothing in pharmacology at all. There are no whole-time teachers in the scientific branches. The professor of anatomy is non-resident.*

His main duty is lecturing, the dissection room being supervised by recent graduates, engaged in practice. 'The professor looks in occasionally.' The professor of pathology is non-resident.

Clinical instruction is given at Portland by teachers who have little commerce with the laboratories in Brunswick. The chief clinical reliance of the school is Maine General Hospital, where instruction is given principally in the amphitheater, as a majority of the cases are surgical. Obstetrical work is not to be counted on. Interns do the clinical laboratory work and make up case histories.

Students spend also a small amount of time at a thoroughly wretched city dispensary, where the cases are few, where no re-cords are kept, and where not even copies of prescriptions are filed. The dispensary does not own a microscope.

A course in clinical microscopy is given at the college building in Portland. 'Urine and sputum are gathered and students are told about the cases from which they come.' Neither end of this school meets the requirements for teaching modern medicine. (9)

With the onset of World War I, Bowdoin College saw a decrease of students and in 1918, the Bowdoin trustees, facing a deficit of $7,000, voted to close the medical school. The board of overseers of the medical school objected to this action but the schools ultimately closed in 1921. (10)

While there were medical practices in Maine as early as 1791, the first statewide organization of Maine physicians, called the Medical Society of Maine, was inaugurated in 1820. In the first year of the separation from Massachusetts, this group met at intervals and in 1834 published its first medical journal. Roads were poor and travel was hard and the soci-ety ceased to meet in 1853. The Maine Medical Association (MMA) was founded on April 28, 1853 when 27 physicians met at the Tontine Hotel in Brunswick, pursuant to a call "addressed to a portion of the medical profession throughout the state." The object of the association was stated to be the promotion of medical service and the regulation of the practice of medicine and surgery in the state. Dr. John McKeen of Topsham was Chairman; Dr. John D. Lincoln, Secretary and Dr. Isaac Lincoln were all elected to serve until the first annual meeting. In its first year members consisted of 82 physicians. On April 28, 2004 a commemorative plaque was placed on the site of the former Tontine Hotel recognizing the 27 physi-cians who founded the MMA exactly 150 years before. At its first annual meeting a code of ethics was adopted, which remains in effect today. (11)

A monument commemorating the founding of the Maine Medical Association, in front of the Tontine Mall, Brunswick, Maine.

THIS MONUMENT COMMEMORATES THE FOUNDING OF THE MAINE MEDICAL ASSOCIATION ON APRIL 28, 1853. ON THAT DATE, AND NEAR THIS SITE, AT WHAT WAS THEN THE TONTINE HOTEL, 27 PHYSICIANS MET TO ORGANIZE THE ASSOCIATION WHICH HAS EXISTED CONTINUALLY TO THIS DAY

DEDICATED APRIL 28, 2003

DR. JAMES MCKEEN, CHAIRMAN
DR. STEPHEN WHITMORE
DR. RICHARD F. JENNESS
DR. JOHN D. LINCOLN
DR. H.H. HILL
DR. G.S. PALMER
DR. ANDREW FULLER
DR. ABIAL LIBBY
DR. ALONZO GARCELON
DR. JOHN BENSON
DR. ISAAC LINCOLN
DR. AMOS NOURSE
DR. CYRUS BRIGGS

DR. ISRAEL PUTNAM
DR. C.W. WHITMORE
DR. ASHUR ELLIS
DR. JOHN MATHEWS
DR. JOSEPH W. ELLIS
DR. CYRUS KENDRICK JR.
DR. GEORGE E. BRICKETT
DR. JOHN HARTWELL
DR. N.R. BOUTELLE
DR. J.F. STANLEY
DR. R.W. LAWSON
DR. J.W. TOWARD
DR. T.G. STOCKBRIDGE
DR. NATHANIEL T. PALMER

3

ORGANIZED HOSPITAL DEVELOPMENT

T HE HISTORY of the hospitals in Bath and Brunswick followed very different path. At the beginning of the 1900s, nowhere in the vicinity of the City of Bath was there a hospital, the nearest being 35 miles away in Portland. As the city had evolved with the success of the shipways, the civic leaders understood modernity. The establishment of the Bath City Hospital was an opportunity to modernize and improve the community. Not only would the hospital attract families to settle near Bath, it would ensure the health of the city, especially if it faced epidemics and disasters.

There is little doubt that the two most notable civic events that occurred in the City of Bath in 1907 were the celebrations of the 300th anniversary of the construction of the little ship *Virginia* by the Popham colonists and the formation of the Bath City Hospital. The Popham colony was an early settlement founded in 1604, located at the mouth of the Kennebec River. Given the celebrations that took place for these two events, the founding of the hospital was not as spectacular as the outpouring of celebrations for the 300th anniversary of the *Virginia;* however, the City of Bath enjoys the benefits of the hospital to this day. (12)

Like other public institutions for the welfare of the Bath community such as homes for the aged and orphans, and the public library, the Bath City Hospital had its origin in the generous public spirited vision of the Bath people themselves. In April 1907, the Honorable John S. Hyde,

SAGADAHOC HISTORY & GENEALOGY ROOM, PATTEN FREE LIBRARY.

SAGADAHOC HISTORY & GENEALOGY ROOM, PATTEN FREE LIBRARY.

1907, the 300th anniversary celebration of the building of the ship Virginia *by Popham colonists.*

then president of the Bath Iron Works, and 109 other prominent citizens addressed a petition to Henry W. Hanson, Justice of the Peace, in the following form:

> "We the undersigned residents of the said county and state desirous of being incorporated pursuant to the provisions of the first, second and third sections of Chapter 57 of the revised statutes of Maine 1903 and acts additional thereto and amendatory thereof, for the purpose of establishing and maintaining in the City of Bath, County and State aforesaid, a suitable hospital for the treatment of general diseases, requests you to issue a warrant directed to one of us, requiring him to call a meeting of these applicants at such time and place as you may appoint that we may then and there organize ourselves into a corporation for the purpose aforesaid, adopt a constitution and bylaws, and transact other business as may properly come before this meeting."

On April 13, 1907, a warrant was issued to Mr. George E. Thompson who then formed a temporary organization the following day. On May 16th the corporation was duly organized by the adoption of bylaws, election of Corporators, and the election of the following officers: President, John S. Hyde; Vice President, Jacob R. Andrews; Secretary, J. Edward Drake; Treasurer, George P. Davenport; Trustees, the President, Secretary and Treasurer ex officio and Denny N. Humphries, Horacio A. Duncan, Galen C. Moses, William D. Sewall, Frank H. Percy, George D. Jackson,

BATH MEMORIAL HOSPITAL
EXPRESSES APPRECIATION OF THE GENEROSITY OF THESE DONORS WHO HAVE LIBERALLY CONTRIBUTED TO THE ENDOWMENT OF THE HOSPITAL

LUCINDA BAILEY	GEORGE P. DAVENPORT	ELLEN S. ROCHE
MARY A. WIGGIN	CORDELIA D. MORRISON	
ADELAIDE E. DELANO	SYDNEY J. MEEKER	
JOHN S. HYDE	EMMA C. GREENLEAF	
EMMA D. SEWALL	CELIA F. LINCOLN	
ARTHUR S. HYDE	DAVID C. MALCOLM	
LUCY W. PATTEN	WILLIAM D. SEWALL	
CHARLES D. CLARKE	ANNA MARY JELLY	
SEAMEN'S FUND	MARY A. SANFORD	
SARAH M. WELLS	GEORGE F. MANSON	
WILLIAM H. SEWALL	MARY E. NUGENT	
MONDAY CLUB	ANNIE E. M. HARRIS	
HAROLD M. SEWALL	ELIZABETH R. MOSES	
E. THERESA MOSES	ALICE W. SEWALL	
SANS SOUCI CLUB	CAMILLA E. A. SEWALL	
ERNESTINE S. WRIGHT	EMMA H. MOSES	
ALBERT H. SHAW	LINA O. SEWALL	
JOSEPH F. SEWALL	MARTHA E. SHAW	

Top: *Bath City Hospital, James Jones Mansion, with new 3-story addition, 1910.*

Lower left: *Bath City Hospital 1912 with new porch.*

Lower right: *Bath Memorial Hospital after 1934*

Sidney J. Meeker, James L. McLennan, Charles W. Clifford, Harold M. Sewall, George E. Hughes and Albert H. Shaw.

The name originally proposed for the institution was Bath General Hospital, but the name adopted and written into the bylaws was Bath City Hospital, as it was known until 1934, when the name was changed to the Bath Memorial Hospital. The change was suggested to honor those individuals from the City of Bath who organized and supported the hospital.

Trustees organized in 1907, to begin the planning of the hospital following the bequest of $5,000 from Lucinda Bailey. The trustees included Bath Iron Works President John Hyde, George Davenport, and Galen Moses. They considered the Lowell Mansion on Oak Street that was a men's home, but were incentivized to move fairly fast because Miss Bailey's money was available for only two years. They decided to purchase the James and Vesta Jones property at the end of the street car line on

Winship Street with 13 rooms and an eight foot wide porch around the house. It was said to have had "excellent sanitary arrangements."

It is not surprising that a controversy ensued over the location of the hospital. Some considered Winship Street too far from the center of the city, taking too long to reach in case of an emergency. Physicians wanted a new building as opposed to a residence and argued it was simply wrong to hurry into spending the money.

Despite the opposition, the hospital opened with six beds in January 1909, with John Hyde, the first president, and Cary Goodrich, the first superintendent.

The three-story brick wing was added to the plans in 1910 increasing the capacity to 36 beds. Over the years several improvements were made, including the addition of the nurses' residence in 1918 and the completion of the maternity ward in 1922 enlarging the capacity to 50 beds. A laundry building was constructed in 1918. The medical reference library was en-

1923 staff and nursing students, Bath City Hospital.

larged from time to time, notably in 1926 and 1931. The X-Ray department was inaugurated in 1925 with new up-to-date X-Ray equipment. The clinical laboratory, with a laboratory technician in charge, and the children's ward were established in 1937.

With the establishment and opening of the hospital in 1909, the medical and surgical staffs were organized. All physicians of the city and several from surrounding towns were invited by the trustees to organize a hospital medical staff which happened on February 9, 1909. Dr. Randall D. Bibber was President and Dr. Franklin A. Ferguson, Secretary, and also included were Drs. Charles A. Packard, James H. Westcott, Adelburke F. Williams, Edwin F. Fuller, Edwin M. Fuller, Jr., William E. Rice, Byron F. Barker, Langdon T. Snipe, Robert T. Donnell, Ebon J. Marston, Horace Fox, Charles F. Curtis, Robert T. Hannigan, Edwin E. Briry, Clarence A. Peaslee and James O. Lincoln.

The Bath Hospital was organized from the outset to be a not-for-profit public institution. It was organized and maintained largely by gifts and bequests of public spirited citizens. A tablet containing the names of the large contributors was placed in the main lobby of the hospital.

MARLA H. DAVIS

THE BATH CITY HOSPITAL TRAINING SCHOOL FOR NURSES

By 1900 nurse training programs were an essential part of hospitals all over the country. They served to provide skills and training for nurses in the home and hospital settings. Just as importantly, they provided an inexpensive, stable, and disciplined workforce. Even the smallest community hospitals started schools for the economic advantage of student labor. Both the Bath Hospital Training School and the Bath City Hospital opened in 1909. The first three students were admitted in 1909 and graduated in the fall of 1912. Courses were entirely lectures given by members of the medical staff. Domestic science was taught by the superintendent. The instruction was probably equivalent to a practical arts course.

In 1940 there were 28 students: eight seniors, four intermediates and 16 juniors. In the last month of training, prior to the cap-

ping exercises, the probationary group of students became intermediate students and eligible for ward assignments. Great efforts were made to stimulate area and regional students to enroll in the school of nursing. The course instruction offered at the training school followed closely the curriculum which had been compiled by nursing educators and adopted as a standard for schools of nursing throughout the country. Upon the completion of training the graduates met minimum requirements of the Maine Board of Registration and were eligible for their RN degree.

Student affiliations included the Children's Hospital in Portland for three months. Here they received instructions and experience in the diseases of children as well as orthopedic instruction. Students were also sent to the Margaret Hague Maternity Hospital in Jersey City, N.J. for three months for their obstetrical training, and to the New Hampshire State Hospital in Concord for training in psychiatric nursing for three months. Massachusetts Eye and Ear Infirmary and the Boston City Hospital were also used as clinical rotation sites.

In 1909 nursing offered one of the few occupational opportunities for women. A nursing education was attractive because there was no cost and prepared the students for independent practice, hospital nursing or administration. The applicants were middle class women from farms and towns. They were local young women or they came from around New England, New Brunswick and Nova Scotia. Based on records compiled over the years, the number of graduates was estimated to be about 200. The school closed in 1947.

1918 The Nurses Home for students was built using, in part, a stable on the property. It faced Winship street. The home was necessary to improve the living conditions and to free up the third floor of the hospital for patients. The home was enlarged in 1927.

The Training School's last class, 1946–47. Left to right: Barbara McKown Pomerleau, Doris Young Watson, Lorna M. Joy, Laura Horne Hodgkins

Graduating Class of 1944–45. Left to right, FRONT *Polly Gagnon Savage, Frances Murphy Smith, Barbary McMann Carlisle, Alma Wasson Lovley and Marion Rose Perkins.* BACK *Althea Cavanaugh Perkins, Beatrice Norton, Marjorie McDonald Voorhees, Jean Nicholson Thayer, Lilly Douglas Foss, Eleanor Bennett Rolfe and Beryl Wheeler Gallant.*

Nursing schools at the time were preoccupied with the moral and social character of students. Older married women were excluded given that they were presumed to have developed a certain autonomy not in keeping with nursing school discipline. They needed a common school education and to present certificates of good moral character. High school education was not required until 1937. This was when minimum standards for nursing education in Maine were imposed. In the early days students were accepted for a two month probation period during which they became familiar with the hospital environment and performed menial, non-direct care tasks for no pay. By 1936 the probation was extended to four months with half the time spent in classroom study and demonstration of nursing skills. If they passed the exam after this period, the students would receive their caps and go on the wards under supervision. Uniforms were an important tool of discipline and identification of class standings in the hierarchy. The heavy blue cotton uniforms with bibs were custom made by the students' mothers. Winter clothing included black stockings. This blue uniform distinguished the students from the graduates who were known as "white nurses."

Working hours for the student nurses were rigorous—12 hour days and a half day off per week. Different shifts were required but classroom work went on in spite of these working conditions. A small stipend of $6 per month was given.

The duration of training was originally two years and was expanded to three years in 1921. This remained the standard of the hospital nursing schools through the 1970s. Ironically few graduate nurses pursued employment in the hospital. The jobs were not there because students took care of the patients. However private duty nurses were employed as common practice at many hospitals including the Bath Hospital. Their pay went to the hospital which in turn paid them.

Discipline controlled every aspect of the student nurse's life. The house mother/superintendent and an instructor were enforcers. The supervisor was considered an autonomous nurse who was subordinate to the board. This role was actually conceived by Florence Nightingale. Two superintendents at the Bath Hospital, Cary Goodwin and Helen Downing, were remembered as strict taskmasters. The nursing school worked with the medical staff to determine the curriculum. The physicians at this time did not believe nurses were capable of learning complex material so the course of study became an apprenticeship consisting of manual skills taught at the bedside. Students also reported that they felt like they had to act like they didn't know anything. Otherwise the physicians might feel that the nurse's knowledge might undermine the patient's faith in the physician.

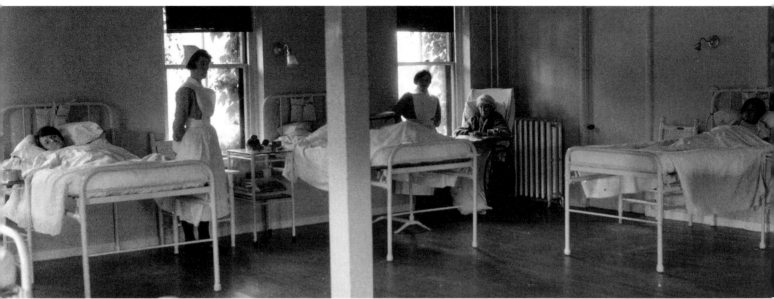

Bath City Hospital circa 1920. The third floor of the brick building was converted to patient care late in 1918. In 1922 it became the maternity unit; likely, women had to be carried up 2 flights.

At the end of the training came graduation and diplomas. Grace Church, then located on Oak Street in Bath was the usual location for the graduation ceremony. Graduates went on to marry, do private duty or work in other hospitals throughout New England and Canada. Bath Hospital established a registry for private duty nurses; patients only had to call the hospital for a nurse's name. The nurse would report to the patient's home and the shift could be as long as 18 hours. These patients were people of means and the only ones who could afford it. (13)

In May 1947 the nurse's training school was closed due to a significant operating deficit. This was precipitated by a reduction of inpatients during World War II when many physicians went off to war. This closing was especially disappointing to the seniors who were transferred to Maine General Hospital in Portland to complete their training.

THE FLU EPIDEMIC

The City of Bath faced its greatest healthcare challenge in 1918 with the onset of the great influenza epidemic. Bath was the epidemic epicenter in Maine as it swept across the country and through the Army both here and overseas with devastating effects. In July, federal, state and city officials, mindful of health risks posed by the surging population, jointly agreed the city should appoint a health officer financed by federal and state funds. Dr. Seth Mullen was appointed the health officer for the city, but nobody imagined a crisis of the magnitude the city was about to face.

On Sept. 25th 1918, an influenza epidemic that would ultimately kill 27 million people worldwide struck Bath. At first, 17 cases were reported, but by noon of Sept. 26th there 47 additional new cases, 15 of them from the crew working on the Emergency Fleet Corporation housing project. Four days later the total number reported in the city had ballooned to 600. By Oct. 8th the number reached 1,800. Another 20 days would pass before the number of newly reported cases dropped into the single numbers.

Because of the government contract work being done at the shipyards, the u.s. Public Health Service stepped in immediately and authorized the Bath mayor, J. Edward Drake, to obtain whatever medical assistance he needed from out of town and to immediately establish an emergency hospital. This was done swiftly by taking over the building that had been established by the Texas Steamship Company at the Kennebec Yacht Club (situated on Front Street just above Grove Street). But it would require three more locations—the Grace Church Parish House at Oak and Middle streets, the Elks Home on Lombard Street and the Winter Street Church Chapel—to handle all of the cases. Nurses and doctors were called from other Maine communities to help staff them. The first 12 days of October, 1918, proved to be the darkest of the epidemic for the eight physicians, 23 nurses and 12 orderlies working in Bath on the payroll of the u.s. Public Health Service. Despite all the efforts, the deadly, Type A flu virus had claimed its first victim—a visiting service man from Massachusetts on September 30th. By mid-October, 40 persons had died in Bath of influenza and pneumonia. By the end of October the epidemic had waned as quickly as it had come only to flare up again during the first nine days of January, 1919. The reported death toll was 55 out of about 2,000 cases in 1918 and another nine out of 320 cases in 1919. The Bath Hospital continued to operate during this period for the general care and emergency care of the people of the area, but efforts were taken to isolate the hospital from patients suffering from the flu. Twenty Red Cross nurses had reinforced the normal nursing forces, and doctors and nurses were engaged in a furious battle to save lives and were working to the limit of their endurance. Three Red Cross nurses working at the yacht club emergency hospital laid down their lives in battle. Harriet Bliss, Bath City Hospital—1915, Alice Dain, Trull Hospital—1922, and Adelaide B. Hogue, Augusta General Hospital—1912, died caring for their patients. There had been many other deaths incidental to the plague and throughout the siege the obituary columns of the local papers were extended to unprecedented lengths. And then the epidemic suspended itself almost as suddenly as it came. (14)

In 1926, Bath City Hospital was accredited by the American College of Surgeons—the forerunner of the Joint Commission for the Accreditation of Hospitals.

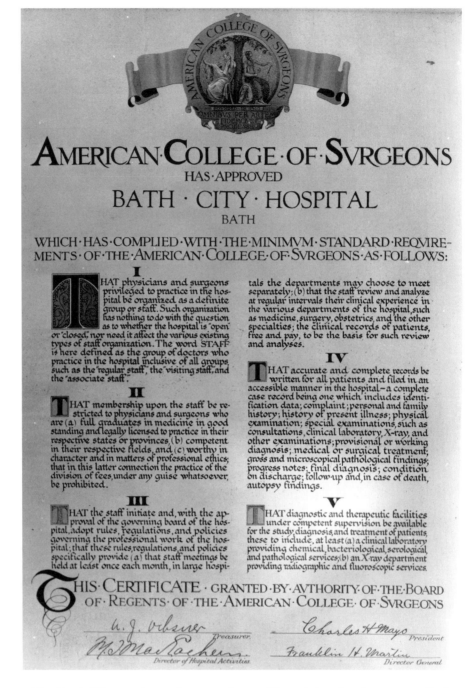

The Bath Hospital was first rated as a Class A by the American College of Surgeons in 1926. It was among the first hospitals in the country to be so accredited. The American College of Surgeons was the forerunner to the Joint Commission on the Accreditation of Hospitals. It was an effort to promote hospital reform based on outcomes in patient care and was the initial attempt to establish hospital standards of care and safety.

From time to time a general appeal to the Bath public was made and the community responded generously. Notably as a result of the ending of

HELP
BLOT OUT
THE
DEBTS
OF THE
HOSPITAL
and place it on a
SOUND
FINANCIAL
BASIS

BATH CITY HOSPITAL
If the Hospital is to continue to do its most efficient work
EVERY ONE MUST HELP

1927 SEPTEMBER 1927						
SUN	MON	TUE	WED	THU	FRI	SAT
				1	2	3
4	5	6	7	8	9	10
11	12	13	14	15	16	17
18	19	20	21	22	23	24
25	26	27	28	29	30	

During the Red Letter Days of September Bath citizens will be asked to subscribe $20,000 to the Loyalty Fund for the Hospital.

BATH CITY HOSPITAL
$20,000
Loyalty Fund Committee

World War I and the diminishing size of Bath Iron Works, the hospital was threatened by a significant decline in its revenues. In a pinch it could raise what it needed, but the hospital continued to be challenged by the growing numbers of patients using its facility. For example in September 1927 the hospital was again at the brink of the financial cliff and launched a "Loyalty Fund" to raise $20,000 and the headline phrase for the campaign was "Save our Hospital." This effort was successful with an all-out effort held between September 12–16, 1927 to raise the needed funds. However, the hospital continued to exist on a shoestring and in 1950 the hospital was at a crossroads of whether to enlarge, to close, or to possibly merge with a larger hospital in another city.

From its founding the Bath Memorial Hospital remained a special interest of Bath's old money families, although it's supporters were by no means restricted to them. As a not-for-profit general care facility, Bath Memorial Hospital was overseen on a volunteer basis by a Board of Trustees and Corporators, some members who gave years of service and financial support. The onset of World War II pushed the economy in Bath to a new peak. The workforce at the Bath Iron Works rose steadily from more than 2,800 by mid-1940 to 4,600 a year later, to more than 12,000 people working three shifts in 1943. The impetus of this was the congressional appropriation in 1940 to build a naval fleet that included 173 destroyers as well as a specific number of battleships, cruisers, aircraft carriers and submarines. BIW would launch four destroyers by the end of 1940, three destroyers and a cargo ship in 1941, 15 destroyers in 1942, 21 destroyers each in 1943 and 1944, and 19 destroyers

This poster helped launch the 1927 fundraising effort—$20,000 was raised in one week for the "Loyalty Fund."

At peak production during WWII, BIW *delivered a destroyer to the Navy every 17 days. Pictured is the* USS Meredith, *which sank off the coast of Utah Beach at Normandy, 1944.*

DD-726
BOW VIEW LOOKING AFT.
BATH, MAINE. DEC. 21 '43

BIW

in 1945. During peak production in 1943–44 the shipyard was turning over a destroyer to the U.S. Navy every 17 days. Each was produced with fewer man hours and fewer defects and a cost 10 to 25% less than the same ships built elsewhere.

The economy of Bath, a hub of commerce at the time for the region, hummed with activity during the World War II years. The city's business district was anchored by four national stores—J. J. Newbury, F. W. Woolworth, W. T. Grant and Sears and Roebuck which had built a new store at the northeast corner of Washington and Center Street in 1941. Also operating out of the downtown area were a half dozen grocery stores including one of the First National chain and one of the A & P chain, two department stores—Senter's and the Bath Department Store, men's clothing stores, 12 beauty parlors, four jewelry stores and nine restaurants among other diverse businesses. At the expense of the federal government,

the infrastructure of the City of Bath had to be increased and improved in order to accommodate the increased population required by the Bath Iron Works. Two housing developments were constructed in 1941 at government expense. Hyde Park Terrace just off Center Street Extension and Lambert Park between High Street and Oak Grove Avenue were built in 1942. In addition to these, dormitories for single workers were constructed on the east side of High Street and additional schools, improved sewers, and other utility work were developed. An elementary school named for Lieutenant John E. L. Huse of Bath, who was killed while serving as a co-pilot on a flying fortress over Java in February 1942, was also built.

Due to increase in population resulting from defense activities it became evident in 1941 that the expansion of the bed capacity of the Bath Memorial Hospital had become an urgent need. Plans were drawn and applications for a grant for the addition were made to the Federal Work

1941 view of Vine Street, Bath. BIW *traffic is lining up to cross the Carlton Bridge.*

Excavation photo published in The Bath Independent, *May 20, 1943. View from Washington Street.*

BUILDING WING ON MEMORIAL HOSPITAL

Agency. Protracted negotiations followed and in March 1942 the trustees of the hospital were notified of the acceptance of a grant in the amount $265,000 for the project. The plans for the wing were held up in June of that year while the government was reconsidering all projects of this nature in the light of the developing scarcity of materials. Revised plans acceptable to the government had to be formed. The hospital addition was ultimately approved by the trustees for construction in September 1942. Alonzo J. Harriman Architects, began work at once on the revised drawings of the wing. Bids for the new hospital were opened in February 1943, and H. P. Cummings Construction Company of Winthrop, Maine won the bid in the sum of $208,690. Construction work was expected to take 12 months, and with this new wing, the hospital became the most modern facility caring for 100 patients. (15)

Over the years the hospital became dependent on members of old money families known as "the silk stocking group" and they were a great reserve for charitable giving. This probably desensitized city politicians to the legitimate needs of public service organizations and the occasional entitlement of such organizations to municipal assistance. The Plant Home, the Bath Memorial Hospital, the Patten Free Library, and the Bath YMCA were all vital parts of the community and were largely dependent on private charities. The hospital volunteers, members of the Board of Trustees and Corporators gave years of service and financial support. (16) The hospital's perennial problem was keeping abreast of medical advances and the increasing demand for its services. Its trustees exhibited great readiness to expand accordingly. The Bath Memorial Hospital's capacity in 1910 was 36 beds. By the end of the bonanza caused by World War I it had grown to

HOSPITAL WING NEARS COMPLETION

In August, 1943 the new wing nears completion. It housed new maternity and pediatric services. Image from August 26, 1943, The Bath Independent.

View of Bath Memorial Hospital in the early 1950s, following the completion of 1943 wing. The new front entrance is at right.

Francis A. Winchenbach
MD, *practiced at* BMH *for 37 years. He was the first medical director.*

50 beds. By the onset of World War II, despite hard times, the hospital had added a clinical laboratory, a maternity ward and X-ray equipment. With the financial support of the federal government the construction of a new wing in 1943 brought the capacity to 100 beds, although that proved to be a mixed blessing. After the war the hospital's physical and financial conditions were so shaky that the influential president of the Board of Trustees, William Newall, President of the Bath Iron Works, recommended that it be closed. This was an unacceptable recommendation for the community. Even though other medical facilities existed in the area, Bath Memorial Hospital had become a source of local pride. Furthermore, its ever increasing usage persuaded many that it was essential to the community's well-being. The hospital struggled on, never far from financial worries, living from year to year on donations from the community.

Rapid transformations were taking place in the internal organization of the hospital. Authority was passing from the trustees to physicians and administrators. Nursing became a trained profession and the direction of medical labor was refined and intensified. The effects of these changes altered the relationship of doctors to hospitals and to one another. The access that private practitioners gained to hospitals without becoming their employees became one of the distinctive features of medical care in American medical activism. Professional dominance and their orientation to the market became widespread and more pronounced.

Bath did not escape this change. Active criticism from the medical staff challenged the Board of Trustees with regard to the operation of the hospital, quality of care, poor financial results and a reduction of patient preference to be hospitalized at the Bath hospital. In response, the board established a special committee to investigate conditions at the hospital and make changes to improve its operation. They sought consultation from Dr. Henry Pollack of Boston, who in turn sent Dr. W. Franklin Wood of Boston to Bath to gather information and make reports to him. (17)

According to the report the conditions of the hospital were due to:

- lack of interest and responsibility on the part of the trustees;

- very cumbersome organization;

- improper and unclear by-laws;

- existing jealousies;

- lack of compliance of the doctors with the by-laws (rules);

- need for role clarification of the professional nurse duties as well as scheduling improvements, and improved cooperation between nursing and training school staff;

- lack of discipline; management was not conducted on a business basis, and;

- poor performance in the kitchen required a dietician.

Dr. Pollock made two essential recommendations:

- Appointment of an administrator who should be a trained executive

- The appointment of a resident physician to assist the medical staff in revisiting standards. (18)

Following these recommendations, Mrs. Wolstenholme, the superintendent of nursing resigned; the size of the Board of Trustees was reduced; the executive committee was given full power and authority to control, manage and operate the hospital (BIW offered to pay the salaries of an administrator, medical director and Director of Nurses—but on the condition that it must approve the appointments to fill the positions. This offer was rejected by the board). (19) Ms. Yellena Seevers, a trained hospital administrator, was hired. Ms. Seevers came from Washington, D.C. where she was Senior Industrial Specialist in the hospital section of the War Production Board. (20) She was trained in hospital administration at the University of Chicago's Program in Hospital Administration. Seevers was given complete charge of the hospital under the supervision of the Executive Committee composed of Chairman W. Dayton Hill, Henry W. Owen, Donald N. Small, Ralph G. Stetson, Archibald M. Main, Mrs. James A. Gillies and Mrs. Frederick E. Drake. The medical staff recommended the appointment of a medical director and Dr. Francis A. Winchenbach was appointed at an annual salary of $4,000. BIW auditors would assist in setting up an efficient accounting system. (21)

In the spring of 1946 there was fierce discussion and division in Congress, and indeed across the country, about a proposed health insurance plan that the Truman administration was bringing forth. While this debate continued the President signed into law one portion of the overall proposal which was known as the Hospital Survey and Construction Act, better known as the Hill-Burton Act. The Legislation had great appeal as a post war reconstruction program and provided economic stimulus and job opportunities for the rebuilding of the hospital systems in the United States. The act provided for an authorization of $75 million a year for five years. Money was distributed to the states which awarded grants based on applications submitted by the hospitals.

4

The COTTAGE HOSPITAL: DEVELOPMENT *in* BRUNSWICK

THE ORIGINAL CONCEPT of a Cottage Hospital was a small rural building or house with several patient beds. The advantage of such a hospital in communities was the provision of local care which avoided long journeys to county or voluntary hospitals. The facilities could deal more immediately with emergencies. Local knowledge of the patient would probably have been lost had they been referred to their nearest county hospital, as was typical for poor patients. The cottage hospitals were usually owned by doctors with no public funds committed to them.

An early cottage hospital in Brunswick was established by Dr. Eva Adams in 1910 where she resided and saw patients in the O'Brien mansion located on the corner of Cumberland and Union Streets until her death in 1929. Little is known about Dr. Adams and her cottage hospital history since it operated as a private business without a Board of Trustees or community advisors. No records of any meetings exist. Dr. Earle Richardson purchased the O'Brien mansion from Dr. Adams in 1926 when he and his family moved from Skowhegan to Brunswick. Dr. Richardson earned his way through college and then made his way through Bowdoin Medical School by thrift and hard work. Dr. Richardson was a quintessential country doctor and was available 24 hours a day. He accepted payment for his services but no one was ever turned away from his small privately owned hospital for lack of money. In 1930 he purchased the second half of the

O'Brien mansion and began a nurse training school. Mrs. Essie Dunlop served as superintendent of nursing and was in charge of the nursing program. The nursing school received many of its students from Canada and had an affiliation with the Boston City Hospital and the Faulkner Hospital in Boston. These affiliations were augmented by nursing training in specialty areas such as obstetrics and medical/surgical nursing.

Dr. Richardson's hospital also served as an emergency room for injured patients and other physicians practicing in town who used it for hospitalized patients. Since both Mr. and Mrs. Dunlop came from New Brunswick, it is more likely the nursing students also came from New Brunswick and eastern Canada. Mrs. Dunlop received her nursing training at the Fordham Hospital in New York, graduating during World War I. The Dunlops maintained an apartment within the hospital. Unfortunately, little is known today about this small training school other than its closure date of 1945. Dr. Richardson operated this hospital until 1946 when he sold it to Dr. Maurice Dionne. The nurses training program was terminated when Dr. Dionne bought the facility. (23)

In 1940 Dr. Clement S. Wilson came to Brunswick following his 1927 graduation from Bowdoin and the completion of his medical training at

1889 announcement for a Cottage Hospital in Brunswick

The O'Brien Mansion located at the corner of Cumberland and Union Street was the cottage hospital of Dr. Eva Adams (1910–1926) when Dr. Earle Richardson purchased the property. It later became the Brunswick Community Hospital operated by Dr. Maurice Dionne.

Doctors Earle Richardson and Maurice Dionne on the occasion of Dr. Richardson's retirement, 1946.

the Yale Medical School in 1931. He purchased the Upham mansion on Park Row, currently the Brunswick Elks Club, and opened his hospital in 1940 with a partner, Dr. Richard Simicheck. Dr. Simicheck left shortly thereafter to enlist in the u.s. Army and Dr. Wilson moved his hospital to 53 Pleasant St. in 1943 where it was known as Dr. Wilson's Hospital. This sixteen-bed facility had one semi-private room, two private rooms and three four-bed wards, an operating room and delivery rooms (at least during World War II). Dr. Wilson's Hospital employed "graduate nurses" who could reside in town or in the nurses home in the east end extension of the building, consisting of three bedrooms, kitchen and living room. The hospital closed early in 1948 shortly after Dr. Wilson died of a cerebral aneurism. A young physician who had joined Dr. Wilson shortly before his death was Dr. Daniel Hanley. He stayed on after Dr. Wilson's death for a short time to oversee the closing of the practice prior to joining Bowdoin College as its physician. Dr. Hanley went on to lead the Maine Medical Society and edit its journal. During his tenure as Bowdoin College physician, he was also named physician to the u.s. Olympic team and developed an international reputation for his work in identifying the use of performance enhancing drugs.

With the purchase of the O'Brien mansion (later known as Brunswick Community Hospital) by Dr. Dionne from Dr. Richardson, the hospital continued to serve the people of Brunswick both for emergency care as well as obstetric and general medical/surgical care. The old three-story Brunswick Community Hospital building stood on the northeast corner of Cumberland and Union streets until the early 1980s as the Brunswick Manor Nursing Home. It was replaced with a new brick structure now called Skolfield House. Around 1940 Dr. Richardson's hospital had twelve private rooms, two semi-private rooms and four wards of four and five beds, as well as operating and delivery rooms, nursery, and laboratories. Because the delivery rooms were on the third floor and walking was the only means of getting there, many women chose to give birth at local "nursing homes."

Alternative facilities for childbirth and post partum care for women in the 1930s, '40s, and '50s included a nursing home on Pleasant street, Topsham, operated by Minnie Griffin; a home at 17 Cleveland St., Bruns-

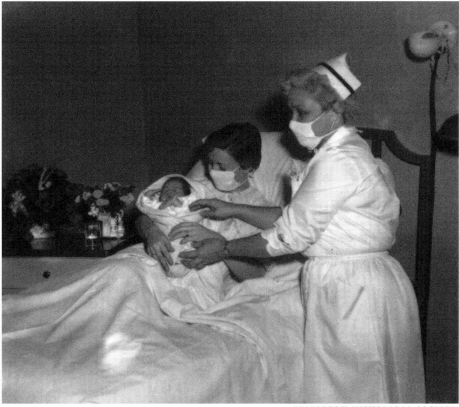

PEJEPSCOT HISTORICAL SOCIETY

wick in the 1930s which might have been the site of an early "hospital" or physician's office apothecary. Mrs. Adams' nursing home at 35 Longfellow St., was very popular with prospective mothers. It was a booming maternity business as many preferred a more homey atmosphere. Mrs. Griffin and Mrs. Adams were both "older women." In the years before managed healthcare and big health insurance companies, childbirth costs were reasonable and manageable regardless of the facility. Local doctors commonly attended deliveries in nursing homes, but sometimes Mrs. Adams delivered the babies, especially when time was short. For a time her daughter assisted. Only two small rooms in the house were assigned to delivery and lying in, which generally lasted 10 days. Although Mrs. Adams was not a graduate nurse, she probably had some nursing training in order to obtain her nursing home license. She attended deliveries in her home into the 1950s. (24)

In 1928 a municipal hospital for contagious diseases was opened. The Burnett farm on the Durham road was established to care for small pox patients. The only evidence of hospital care in Topsham was the short lived Barrow's Hospital at 11 Winter Street which was opened in 1937 by Dr. Vernon H. Lowell. It likely closed in 1939 when it disappeared from the city directory. (25)

In the mid-1950s it became clear that Brunswick needed a modern hospital. The town had been served well by the Brunswick Community Hospital but a modern facility was needed.

Dr. Dionne recognized that private ownership was not sustainable for a growing community and had the foresight to change the name to Brunswick Community Hospital in 1955, and to establish it as a not-for-profit, voluntary general hospital. With this change a community Board of Trustees came into existence, serving as a sounding board for services the hospital provided, and also serving to identify the unmet needs of the community. As a result, several members of that board resigned in the mid '50s to explore the feasibility of building a new, not-for-profit community hospital. They were Avery Fides, Mrs. F. Webster Browne, Paul K. Niven, and Mrs. Herbert White. A tacit agreement was made that at such time as a new hospital became a reality, the Brunswick Community Hospital would close. The organizing committee for the new hospital held its first meeting on May 7, 1957, and attending were Mr. Niven as presiding officer, Henry N. Baribeau, Mrs. Browne, Merle F. Goff (Town Manager of Brunswick), Mrs. White, Harry G. Shulman, Philip S. Wilder, J. A. Aldred, and H. A. Waldkoening. Mr. Aldred was designated as legal counsel and was authorized to proceed with the incorporation. (26)

Serving as incorporators and directors were Mr. Niven, Mrs. Browne, Mr. Goff, Mr. Shulman, Mr. Baribeau and Mr. Fides. Mr. Wilder was named fund campaign chairman and was instructed to ask people he had enlisted to date to continue in their respective capacities in the campaign to raise funds for the new hospital. The initial board of directors comprised James Black, John Baxter, Adjuter E. Contreau, Paul Powers, Mrs. J. J. Morin, Allen Morrell, Ellis L. Aldrich, H. Leighton Jackson, Lloyd A. E. Livesay, Col. Oramel H. Stanley, Russell S. Douglas, William H. Farrar, Samuel L. Forsaith, Richard Hatch, Brice Booker, Mrs. Thomas P. Riley, Raoul Busque, Walter Kling, Vining C. Dunlap, Samuel A. Ladd, Jr. plus the organizing committee previously named. On May 28, 1957 Regional Memorial Hospital was incorporated.

5

The TRAVESTY *of* PLANNING: OPPORTUNITIES LOST

THE PRESIDENT of the Board of Trustees of the new hospital, Avery M. Fides, contacted the University of Vermont Medical School, Department of Health Studies, requesting its assistance in conducting an unbiased study and report to identify the hospital needs of the Brunswick community and to develop a rational approach for moving ahead. The cost of preparing this report was funded by the Commonwealth Fund, a not-for-profit privately endowed trust. This study was made by a group of distinguished researchers thoroughly qualified by experience to investigate and make recommendations. Leading the study group was Leon R. Lazer, PhD. The study logically looked at the regional needs and incorporated Bath demographics.

In 1954 Dr. Ronald A. Bettle, a surgeon associated with the Seventh Day Adventist Church, moved to Brunswick to begin the practice of surgery. During the mid 1950s Dr. Bettle also had recognized the need for expanded and improved hospital facilities and through his efforts the Seventh Day Adventists began planning for an Adventist hospital to be built in Brunswick. This plan ignored the efforts of the University of Vermont study that was underway. The Adventist hospital would be based on the concept of health education and wellness promotion, which was a prominent part of the Seventh Day Adventist philosophy along with providing medical/surgical and emergency care.

Ronald A. Bettle, MD

According to the final report of the University of Vermont dated November 21, 1957 the following details were reported:

With the two groups working independently there was no focused leadership to develop a rational plan for the region. According to the study being conducted by the University of Vermont researchers, it was reasonably certain that two hospitals would not survive, or if they did, they would barely survive with the population to be served. It became clear about the time of the survey that there was continuous conflict of purpose so far as the community was concerned, with two groups trying to establish a hospital. One of the first endeavors was to determine whether or not there was an actual community split on the question of who should build a hospital. It was established that there was no real community split on the question but there was a great deal of interest in the duplicated attempts to "get there first." The University of Vermont researchers called a meeting of the leadership of Parkview Memorial Hospital, Regional Memorial Hospital, the Brunswick Community Hospital and the Chamber of Commerce to stop the Parkview planning until the University of Vermont project was completed and recommendations made. According to the document reporting the results of the study there was a meeting held on Aug. 17, 1957 when all parties agreed there would be no further attempt at promoting hospital interests until the University of Vermont was completed. In the light of this kind of unselfish concern for the best interest of the community it seemed possible to proceed with a lengthy study that would not be biased by intervening propaganda from any side. However, the Parkview Hospital and Sanatorium repeatedly abrogated this agreement by sending out propaganda to a mailing list. Responsibility for this can be taken only by the Parkview Hospital and Sanatorium board. This continued campaign through the mails in spite of the agreement of Aug. 17, 1957 went out over the signature of the Chairman of the Board and the Secretary/Treasurer

1960 Building and Development Committee. Left to right: Raymond Small, Duncan McInness, Donald Burkhardt and G. Baer Connard.

CARING FOR OUR COMMUNITIES

of the board in at least two instances. The study group considered this a serious thing and interpreted as a purely selfish motive. The agreement reached on Aug. 17th would have, if kept, demonstrated genuine community interest. It should be pointed out that the Parkview Hospital and Sanatorium trustees do not represent the community as a whole. For the most part the trustees lived beyond the bounds of the logical areas to be served by the hospital. (27)

The study group made five major recommendations:

- That there be one general hospital for the Bath/Brunswick area

- That the general hospital encompass health services for the community as a whole and should include a division of medical services to meet acute medical and ambulatory needs.

- Consideration should be given to patient facilities geared to the health education and specialty clinics

- That this hospital be located at a point between Bath and Brunswick but not necessarily equally distant from the center of the two communities; that this hospital be established, owned and operated by a board of trustees representative of the area as a whole

- That the cost of building and equipping the hospital should be shared by the federal government through the Hill Burton Program which provided construction funding for community hospitals and by charitable foundations, thus considerably reducing the amount needed from the two communities for the construction. (28)

Emergency entrance of Bath Memorial Hospital 1960

The study recognized the trend of hospitalization, problems in the economy of operation, as well as the importance of understanding contiguous areas in order to interpret needs more accurately which made it necessary to include Bath and the surrounding area.

At a meeting held on March 11, 1957 at the Bath Memorial Hospital, representatives from Bath and Brunswick met to discuss the consultant's report and the possible combined efforts to build a single hospital unit midway between the two communities. The final decision by Bath was not to join with Brunswick in this ef-

fort although there was considerable discussion about the issue and a suggestion was made to consider building the new 50-bed hospital near Bath giving some thought as to the possibility of a merger in the future. However, no action was taken on this suggestion. This became a highly charged emotional discussion among the trustees of the Bath Hospital. Many felt that Bath was a regional pacesetter with its history of time honored traditions in the shipbuilding industry and that a merger with Brunswick was unacceptable. In 1958 after an architectural review of the Bath Hospital, the board launched a $400,000 drive to fund a 32-bed wing that grew into an expanded project of 64 beds in October of 1960. (29) These funds raised in the community were matched by a Hill Burton grant with further support coming from the Ford Foundation. (22) The Brunswick group looked for a more local site.

1960 BUILDING AND DEVELOPMENT PROGRAM TO ENLARGE AND MODERNIZE BATH MEMORIAL HOSPITAL

To demonstrate the need for proceeding with the 1960 expansion of the Bath hospital, the theme of the public relations material was "One in Every Seven," with the campaign brochure relating that in 1957 one in every seven Bath area residents sought treatment at Bath Memorial Hospital. Participation in health plans had led to "over-crowding" above the 63 beds (placing patients in solarium and hallways) and an average daily census was 79% of hospital capacity. (By today's models of determining the need for growth, this census data hardly confirms that the area was under-bedded. It is unclear what efforts, if any, were instituted to even

This photo covered the BMH *"One in Every Seven" Campaign booklet. Left to right: Rowland Farnham, Howard Mayo, Eddie Nabor, and Kate Libby* RN.

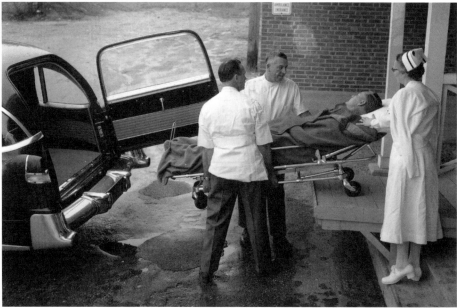

MAINE MARITIME MUSEUM

CARING FOR OUR COMMUNITIES

out the demand for admission.) The brochure outlines the increases seen over the 1947-1957 decade including increases in operations, births, X-rays outpatient visits and lab tests.

Capital campaign funds were also used to upgrade the 1909 building to bring business functions together, raze the Jones Mansion, and install a new coffee shop.

In Brunswick discussions took place between the group that had been incorporated to form a not-for-profit community hospital and Dr. Bettle regarding the role that each facility might play in the community. At one point there appeared to be an agreement that the Parkview Hospital's mission would be based primarily on the rehabilitation aspects of the patient, the spirit, the mind and the body, and that the community hospital would be an acute care facility.

In a communication dated Oct. 3, 1956 between Dr. Bettle and Dr. Weaver, another Seventh Day Adventist physician practicing in the area, Dr. Bettle shared a draft of a joint agreement which had been drafted by both the Parkview and the Regional Memorial Hospital groups in preparation for a meeting to be held later in the month. The joint agreement was as follows:

Preparing the construction site of the 1960 BMH *wing included razing the Jones Mansion. The wing housed 64 beds bringing hospital capacity to 100 beds.*

"The boards of trustees of the Brunswick Community Hospital and Parkview Sanitarium have collaborated in developing plans for health and hospital facilities to serve the community. The two boards had unanimously agreed to plan the fundraising, building and integration of these units so there would be no unnecessary duplication of services or efforts."

The overall plan called for the construction of two new hospital units. First, a new general hospital to be operated by the Regional Memorial Hospital board, and second, a new convalescent and rehabilitation center to be operated by the Parkview Hospital and Sanitarium board.

The specific agreements are as follows:

1. The Brunswick Community Hospital trustees planned to build a hospital to include surgery, obstetrics, emergency services and diagnostic facilities with 50 beds. The estimated cost is $800,000, of which $550,000 is to be raised by a community campaign and $250,000 is expected to be provided by a grant from the Federal Government under the Hill Burton Act. Because of the urgent need, the campaign to secure the $550,000 needed for the Community Hospital will be conducted first. Preliminary work on this effort will begin immediately and is expected to be completed by the end of August 1957.

2. The Parkview Sanitarium Board plans to build a 25-bed convalescent and rehabilitation center. In this unit emphasis will be on the restoration of the chronically ill and handicapped to the fullest physical, mental, social, vocational, and economic usefulness of which they are capable. It is estimated that this unit will cost $160,000 of which $85,000 is to be raised by the community campaign which will be started Sept. 1, 1957 following the Community Hospital campaign.

3. Both boards have agreed to fully support each fundraising effort. In order to carry out the program, a joint committee of representatives of each board will be formed.

4. Construction of both facilities will proceed as rapidly as funds are available.

5. The present general hospital will continue to be operated by the board of trustees of the Brunswick Community Hospital until the new general hospital is built and in operation. Thereafter, the community hospital would be converted into a home for the elderly. No funds described in the community fundraising effort will be used in its acquisition or operation, it is expected to be self-supporting. (30)

RMH *architectural drawing, 1958*

Hospital Gets Deed

"Mitchell Cope, seated left, president of the Minat Corporation of Portland... turned over to Avery M. Fides, president of the Regional Memorial Hospital, Inc. of Brunswick, the deed for land near Bowdoin Park which will be used as a site for a new hospital. Looking on are James Saunders of Portland, architect for the 50-bed hospital; Walter L. Kling of Harpswell, treasurer, and Donald M. Parks, attorney for the Regional group. The land, approximately eight acres, is a gift from the Minat Corporation. (By Staff Photographer Shulman)"
—The Brunswick Record

This fundamental understanding held until a meeting took place between three officials from Loma Linda, CA, which was the center of the Adventist healthcare system and Dr. Ronald Bettle and the Regional Memorial Hospital group. The Adventist officials indicated that it was their intent to build an acute general hospital in Brunswick recognizing it would be in competition with the Regional Memorial Hospital. Thus, the joint agreement was ignored, and the two hospitals opened within months of one another, less than a fifth of a mile apart. (31) Competition has existed between the two facilities since 1959. The Seventh Day Adventist Hospital, known as Parkview Memorial Hospital, has been controlled by the Adventist Church officials and the predominant number of physicians associated with Parkview have been Loma Linda University graduates. Shortly after the opening of the Parkview Hospital, Dr. Bettle was reassigned to the new Hackensack, N.J. Adventist Hospital as chairman of the Health Education Committee. (32)

THE BEGINNING OF REGIONAL MEMORIAL HOSPITAL
Mitchell Cope of Portland, president of the Minot Corporation, donated eight acres of land for the future hospital. He had built several housing developments in Brunswick including the homes located on Peary and MacMillan Drives adjacent to the land he was donating. Seeking funding under the provisions of the Hill-Burton Act was a Regional Memo-

rial Hospital delegation of President James S. Coles of Bowdoin College and John L. Baxter, a prominent Brunswick citizen and a member of the board of directors of the hospital. They presented Regional's application to a committee of Maine physicians charged with the responsibility of allocating federal funds under the Hill-Burton Act. Federal Aid in the amount of $361,000 was awarded to Regional Memorial Hospital. Greatly encouraged by the gift of land and by the grant of federal funds, Regional trustees set about the solicitation of further contributions to the building fund. Phillip S. Wilder served as chairman of the fundraising committee. The trustees showed their faith and set a splendid example by making generous initial gifts. Residents of nine communities volunteered for an arduous task of asking for money for the new hospital. Contributions of $100 or more were awarded certificates designating those contributors as hospital founders. The names of all founders were inscribed on a plaque which hangs in a prominent place in Mid Coast Hospital today. Other generous gifts memorialized or honored individuals by naming individual spaces within the hospital.

The Brunswick *Times Record* reported, "The opening of the Regional Memorial Hospital in November 1960 was the fruition of the hope, the plans, the sustained hard work and the generosity of hundreds of dedicated people—men and women—of the town and communities surrounding Brunswick. In combination these efforts represented perhaps the greatest local community enterprise in the 20th century, undoubtedly one of the most heartening and rewarding activities engaged in during the lifetime of those involved."

Regional Memorial Hospital, Brunswick

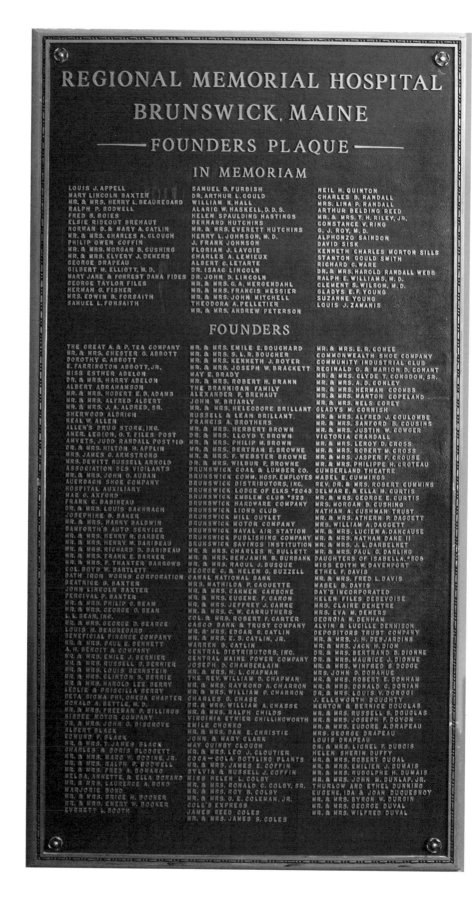

REGIONAL MEMORIAL HOSPITAL

BRUNSWICK, MAINE

— FOUNDERS PLAQUE —

FOUNDERS

MR. & MRS. LOUIS A. DYE	MR. & MRS. CLARENCE M. HALEY	MRS. JOSEPHINE C. LAVOIE
MR. & MRS. C. CABOT EASTON	MR. & MRS. HERBERT L. HALL	MR. & MRS. PIERRE J. LAVOIE
MILDRED F. EDWARDS	MR. & MRS. WILLIAM K. HALL	MR. & MRS. ERVIN C. LEATHERS
MR. & MRS. EARL A. ELKINS	MR. & MRS. CHARLES W. HAM	MRS. ALMA LEBEL
MR. & MRS. GILBERT M. ELLIOTT	MR. & MRS. EDWARD S. HAMMOND	JOEL P. & ROSE C. LEBEL
MR. & MRS. NORMAN EMERSON	THE DANIEL F. HANLEY FAMILY	MR. & MRS. LAVAL R. LEBEL
EMILE THE TAILOR	MR. & MRS. W. E. HANNAFORD	MR. & MRS. ELMER A. LEBLANC
ENDICOTT—JOHNSON SHOE COMPANY	MR. & MRS. M. STANLEY HANSCOM	FRANK D. LEBLANC
MR. & MRS. STEPHEN M. ETNIER	HARRASEEKET GRANGE * 9	MR. & MRS. LOUIS H. LEBLOND
FARNSWORTH MILL	MR. & MRS. JAMES HARVIE	MR. & MRS. CONRAD LEBOURDAIS
ERMA C. FARRAR	ALARIC W. HASKELL	MR. & MRS. GEORGE LEBOURDAIS
WILLIAM H. FARRAR	HENRY C. HASKELL	MISSES ZOE & HELENE LEBOURDAIS
D. A. FAVREAU & SONS	MR. & MRS. J. MURRAY HASTINGS	MR. & MRS. GUSTAVE O. LECLAIR
MR. & MRS. DONAT A. FAVREAU	MR. & MRS. MALCOLM D. HATCH	MRS. VICTORIA BECHARD LECLAIR
MR. & MRS. RAYMOND J. FAVREAU	KARL D. & GRETCHEN A. HATCH	ALMOZA C. LECLERC
FEDERAL DISTRIBUTORS, INC.	MR. & MRS. RICHARD L. HATCH	MR. & MRS. CHARLES E. LECLERC
MR. & MRS. AVERY M. FIDES	MRS. WILFORD J. HAWKINS	MISS LILLIAN LEFEBVRE
MR. & MRS. A. W. FIDES, JR.	MRS. ALBERT W. HAYWARD	DR. & MRS. ROBERT F. LEGENDRE
MRS. FORREST D. FIDES	MARY F. HAZELL	MR. & MRS. EATON LEITH
MR. & MRS. HERMAN L. FIELD	MR. & MRS. KEVIN HEBERT	HELEN M. LESLIE
DRUSILLA FIELDING	JOSEPH I. HELIE	MR. & MRS. JOHN F. LESLIE
MR. & MRS. ANDREW A. FIORI	MR. & MRS. E. C HELMREICH	MR. & MRS. CLYDE LESURE
MR. & MRS. COLUMBUS FIORI	MR. & MRS. FREDERICK J. HENNARD	MRS. ALBERT L. LETARTE
THE J. A. FIORI FAMILY	MR. & MRS. EDWARD V. HENNESSEY	LEWIS INDUSTRIAL BUILDING
FIRST—AUBURN TRUST COMPANY	MR. & MRS. JOHN H. HENSHAW	MR. & MRS. RICHARD B. LEWSEN
FIRST NATIONAL BANK, BRUNSWICK	REV. JAMES E. HERRICK	MR. & MRS. THOMAS M. LIBBY
FIRST NATIONAL STORES	CAPT. & MRS. ELMER R. HILL	C. S. F. LINCOLN
FIRST PORTLAND NATIONAL BANK	MR. & MRS. FRANK HILL, JR.	CARL & MARY LINSCOTT
EUGENE & RUTH FISHER	MR. & MRS. ERNEST HILLMAN	LISBON TRADING POST
MR. & MRS. LAWRENCE N. FISHER	EDNA L. HODSDON	MRS. NEAL M. LITCHFIELD
MR. & MRS. AUGUSTINE S. FITTS	MR. & MRS. WILLIAM D. HOFFMAN	MR. & MRS. LEO LIVERNOIS
AGNES R. FORD	FRANCES & WOLCOTT HOKANSON	MR. & MRS. C. H. LIVINGSTON
SAMUEL L. FORSAITH	BRIG. GEN. A. B. HOLMES	WILLIAM N. & ANTOINETTE LOCKE
ISABEL S. FORSAITH	EMILY B. HOLMES	DR. G. E. C. LOGAN
MR. & MRS. EUGENE A. FORTIN	MR. & MRS. ARCHIE W. HOLMES	MR. & MRS. ALBERT O. LORD
MR. & MRS. FREDERIC E. FORTIN	MR. & MRS. CECIL T. HOLMES	MR. & MRS. ANTONIO S. LORD
MISS GLORIA S. FORTIN	H. P. HOOD & SONS, BRUNSWICK	MR. & MRS. HUGH C. LORD
MR. & MRS. JOSEPH F. FORTIN	MR. & MRS. ORREN C. HORMELL	JOSEPH FORTUNAT LORD
LEON J. FORTIN	DR. GORDON R. HOWARD	MR. & MRS. HERBERT E. LUBEE
MR. & MRS. VICTOR L. FORTIN	MRS. HARVEY HOWARD	MR. & MRS. EVERETT M. LUNT
MR. & MRS. REMILDO R. FORTINI	ELEANOR T. HOWE	DR. & MRS. CHEEVER J. LYDEN
ROY A. FOULKE	MR. & MRS. HARRISON W. HUBBARD	EDITH E. LYON
MR. & MRS. BERTRAND FOURNIER	MR. & MRS. C. E. HUNTINGTON	MR. & MRS. MERLE A. MACDONALD
DR. & MRS. WILLIAM H. FOX	MRS. BENJAMIN INGALLS	MR. & MRS. J. V. A. MACKENZIE
FREEPORT FUEL & GRAIN COMPANY	MR. & MRS. WILLIAM D. IRELAND	DR. & MRS. DONALD MACOMBER
FREEPORT SHOE COMPANY	DR. & MRS. MAYNARD M. IRISH	JOHN J. MAGEE
MR. & MRS. RAYMOND A. FREEMAN	J. & J. CLEANERS	THE MAHANEY COMPANY
MR. & MRS. RUSSELL A. FRENCH	MR. & MRS. JOHN L. JACK	MAINE SAVINGS BANK
THE FRIENDSHIP CLUB	MR. & MRS. GEORGE JARVIS	RALPH MAIRS
MR. & MRS. ALLAN C. FRIZZLE	JAY CORPORATION EMPLOYEES	MRS. RALPH A. MALLETT
JOHN W. FROST	MR. & MRS. MYRON A. JEPPESEN	MR. & MRS. LEO MARCHILDON
MRS. GEORGE B. FUNDENBURG	IVA CATLIN JEWELL	MARIST FATHERS
MRS. EDITH M. FURBISH	HELEN B. JOHNSON	MARY & SEWARD MARSH
MR. & MRS. ARTHUR A. GAGNE	MRS. HENRY L. JOHNSON	MR. & MRS. JAMES N. MARSHALL
ELMER J. GAY	JESSE M. JOHNSON	MR. & MRS. LOUIS MARSTALLER
WILLIAM D. GEOGHEGAN	PHILIP H. JOHNSON	MR. & MRS. OVILA E. MARTIN
ERNEST & LAZARINE GEORGE	PHILIP R. JOHNSON	MADELEINE M. MASSE
GEORGE'S AMOCO STATION	MR. & MRS. WILFORD E. JONES	MR. & MRS. ROBERT J. MASSE
MR. & MRS. STAN GERVAIS	MRS. RALPH L. JORDAN	MR. & MRS. ROLAND F. MASSE
EVERETT L. GILES	DR. & MRS. SANFORD KAMINESTER	MR. & MRS. DONALD R. MATHIESON
GILLMAN MUSIC COMPANY, INC.	MR. & MRS. RALPH KEENAN	MABEL N. MATTHEWS
MR. & MRS. ROBERT H. GLOVER	KEENAN'S JENNEY SERVICE STATION	ALICE E. MAXWELL
MERLE F. & RUTH F. GOFF	MR. & MRS. N. C. KENDRICK	GEORGE O. MAY
F. J. GOSSELIN & SONS	MR. & MRS. CHARLES KILBRIDE	MR. & MRS. HARRY S. MCCARTHY
RAOUL F. GOSSELIN	MR. & MRS. E. STANLEY KITCHIN	MR. & MRS. CONRAD MCDUFF
ROLAND H. GOSSELIN	MR. & MRS. WALTER L. KLING	MR. & MRS. NUMA J. MCDUFF
RUTH R. GOSSELIN	KNIGHTS OF COLUMBUS	DR. & MRS. CURRIER MCEWEN
MRS. ARTHUR L. GOULD	KNIGHTS OF PYTHIAS	MR. & MRS. AARON P. MCFARLAND
MR. & MRS. CHARLES S. GOULD	MR. & MRS. FRITZ C. A. KOELLN	EDWARD A. MCFARLAND, M. D.
MISS EDNA GOULD	MRS. GERTRUDE KOREVA	MR. & MRS. RALPH A. MCINTIRE
MR. & MRS. GARDNER S. GOULD	MR. & MRS. REINHARD L. KORGEN	HAZEL C. MCKEE
MR. & MRS. PERLEY E. GOWELL	DONALD NASH KOUGHAN	REV. & MRS. HORACE M. MCMULLEN
GRANITE FARM DAIRY	MISS SHEILA JOAN KOUGHAN	FRANK MCWILLIAMS
W. T. GRANT & COMPANY	CARL SMITH KUEBLER	MR. & MRS. H. E. MEHLHORN
ARLETTA BREHAUT GRAVES	JOSEPH T. LACHANCE	LUCY H. MELCHER
MR. & MRS. A. LEROY GREASON	MARIE ANNE LACHANCE	WILLIAM CAREY MELOY
EDITH C. GREENE	RUSSELL G. LACHANCE	EDNA A. MENZIES
MR. & MRS. LAWRENCE H. GREGSON	MR. & MRS. BERTRAND LACHARITE	C. H. MERGENDAHL & FAMILY
MR. & MRS. ERNEST R. GRIFFIN	MRS. RAE Y. LACROIX	ARTHUR S. MERRILL
GEORGE C. GRIFFING	ESTELLE H. LADD	MR. & MRS. BERT D. MERRILL
DR. & MRS. ALFRED O. GROSS	SAMUEL A. LADD, JR.	MERRILL TRANSPORT COMPANY
ALFRED & EVELYN GROTE	SAMUEL A. LADD III	MR. & MRS. LAWRENCE MERRIMAN
STANLEY GRUMBACHER FOUNDATION	HARRY W. & DORIS S. LALLY	MR. & MRS. RAY MERRIMAN
GUARDIAN LOAN COMPANY	MR. & MRS. D. D. LANCASTER	SHUBAEL H. MERRIMAN
MR. & MRS. ALFRED N. GUINARD	A. J. LANGFORD	MERRYMEETING MEDICAL GROUP
MR. & MRS. ELTON D. GULLIFER	MR. & MRS. PAUL M. LANGLEY	MR. & MRS. HENRY C. MESSIER
MR. & MRS. ROY V. GUPTILL	MRS. SARAH B. LANGLEY	JULIETTE MESSIER
MR. & MRS. ALTON H. GUSTAFSON	LOUISE LAPOINTE	MR. & MRS. R. E. MICHAUD
HAROLD G. HAGGETT		MR. & MRS. HENRY MILLIKEN

Regional Memorial Hospital opened its doors with a 55-bed acute care hospital in 1960. Louis Dye was hired as the first administrator. Dye had been responsible for running the clinic at Brunswick Naval Air Station and had some training in hospital administration while in the military.

There was a growing recognition that there was an unmet need in the community for long term/rehabilitation beds. Dr. Daniel Hanley, President of the medical staff, emphasized the critical need for a new wing for the chronically ill. In an effort to best utilize the resources of the community, Avery Fides, chairman of the Regional board of trustees, again approached the Parkview Hospital leadership with a proposal to convert their beds into a rehabilitation center for the chronically ill. This request was first proposed in 1957 when the two hospitals were in the planning stages. Parkview again rejected this proposal in a letter from Carl P. Anderson, Chairman of the Parkview board dated May 21, 1964. The responsible board of trustees of Parkview was known as the Membership Committee and was appointed by and made up of the leadership of the Northern New England Conference of Seventh Day Adventists, whose offices were located in Portland. No local trustee responsibility for decision making existed at Parkview.

This organizational structure highlighted the classic struggle between the trustees who govern the community hospital with the trustees of the faith based hospital. One directed primarily toward the unmet needs of the community; the other whose decision making supports the needs of the church.

The trustees of Regional, recognizing the need for long term rehabilitation beds, proceeded with construction of a 22-bed rehabilitation unit dedicated in 1966. Trustees knew a major unrestricted bequest to Regional from the estate of Ralph Bodwell of about $775,000 was in the process of being probated. Price of the new wing was $525,000; a decision was made to request $200,000 from the Hill-Burton Fund and the remaining $325,000 would come from the Bodwell estate. The new wing would be designated as the Bodwell Unit. Other major accomplishments at Regional were accreditation by the Joint Commission in 1963, completion of the Intensive Care Unit in 1969 and updating of the Radiology and Laboratory departments. A 22-bed Psychiatric inpatient and day care facility was opened in 1973 and the seven-bed Children's Unit in was opened in 1974 as a result of a gift from May Quinby Clough "for the children of the community." The Medical Office Building adjacent to Regional was acquired from Dr. Maurice Dionne in 1977.

May Quinby Clough with nurse Sharon Newbern and patient Tia Travierso, age 7, circa 1974.

CLOUGH CHILDREN'S UNIT
MADE POSSIBLE
BY THE GENEROUS GIFT OF
MISS MAY QUINBY CLOUGH
DEDICATED TO THE CHILDREN
OF THE COMMUNITY
1973

Nancy "Ginger" Smith

*Regional Memorial
Hospital circa 1982*

TROUBLE ERUPTS AT REGIONAL MEMORIAL HOSPITAL

Late in 1976 leadership struggles began to erupt, resulting in a power/authority conflict between the director of nursing Jean Caron, RN, and the chief of obstetrics Dr. Rudolph Winklebauer. The administrator, Robert R. Petit failed to resolve the conflict in a timely manner and as a result, the chief of obstetrics left Regional and started to admit his patients to Parkview.

Dr. Winklebauer, an authoritarian figure, had neglected to build his department for the future and did not recruit any OB/GYN colleagues to Regional. As a result of his move to Parkview, Regional was left with only a small number of general practitioners delivering a limited number of babies. Trustees voted to close the obstetrical service and terminated both the administrator and director of nursing. Richard Ziegler was named acting administrator and Nancy "Ginger" Smith, RN was named acting director of nursing.

Herbert Paris, then associate director of Yale New-Haven Hospital, in Connecticut was recruited and named administrator of Regional in 1978. Paris enjoyed a wide reputation nationally that went beyond his leadership in the New Haven community. At Yale New-Haven Hospital he served as the associate director, and also director of ambulatory services for both the hospital and Yale Medical School. He provided the leadership for the hos-

pital's role in developing primary care services to the community and was the leader in developing a centralized emergency response system for a 21-community area, including the development and training of emergency medical technicians. Additionally, he maintained a teaching position at Yale University and Yale Medical School. Shortly after Paris arrived in Brunswick, he recruited Lester Hodgdon to become the chief financial officer. Hodgdon was recognized as one of the leading hospital financial officers in Connecticut, coming from Watertown Hospital. Nancy "Ginger" Smith who had been in an acting role of director of nursing was appointed director of nursing.

Herbert Paris

Numerous problems faced Regional at this time. There was a lack of support by the medical staff to re-establish obstetrics. The physical facilities represented the inefficient design of the pavilion style architecture present in hospitals designed in the late 1940s and early '50s. So, in 1980 the hospital purchased 30 acres of additional land next to the existing hospital and in 1981 proceeded to undertake the first modernization project at Regional. A new two story wing provided more than 20,000 square feet of needed space. The emergency room and outpatient treatment areas were to occupy the first floor, with a new main entrance and an emergency entrance. The second floor contained four enlarged operating suites and supportive areas. The space vacated by the old operating suites, emergency room and outpatient treatment areas were converted for several departments to allow for enlargement and modernization and centralized storage. Construction began in the spring of 1981 at a cost of $4 million. The architect was John Wilson of Payette Associates of Boston and building contractor was H. P. Cummings under the direction of Dallas Folk. A successful fundraising campaign under the leadership of W. Streeter Bass exceeded its goal. Shortly after the opening of the new expansion a local artist and bird carver, Charles Greenough Chase, provided a gift to memorialize his late wife, Doris Marie Ahlers Lojahn-Chase, a hospital architect and friend of Regional, with a dedication garden on a knoll next to the front entrance. The slate plaque mounted on a huge boulder has the inscription "devoted to patient comfort through good design."

John Wilson, Richard A. Morrell and Herbert Paris

REGIONAL MEMORIAL HOSPITAL
25TH ANNIVERSARY

MEMBERS OF THE ACTIVE MEDICAL STAFF

1960–1985

John B. Anderson, M.D.
Louis Bachrach, M.D.
Lawrence W. Bailey, D.O.
Kirk K. Barnes, M.D.
Michael Barton, M.D.
Ronald A. Bettle, M.D.
John S. Bisgrove, M.D.
Nelson P. Blackburn, M.D.
Robert B. Bokat, M.D.
Sunny J. Bullington, M.D.
Robert S. Carson, M.D.
Manu Chatterjee, M.D.
Kenneth H. Clark, M.D.
Marilyn R. Clark, M.D.
Michael T. Contartese, M.D.
Andrew D. Cook, M.D.
Philip S. Crichton, M.D.
Charles S. Crummy, M.D.
G. H. Darakjian, M.D.
Eduardo E. Darcy, M.D.
Maurice J. Dionne, M.D.
Robert H. Dixon, M.D.
Raymond H. Dominici, M.D.
Louis V. Dorogi, M.D.
Peter A. Evans, M.D.
Richard Evans, III, M.D.
James L. Fife, M.D.
Robert S. Galen, M.D.
Maurice Ghaly, M.D.
Richard A. Giustra, M.D.
Floyd B. Goffin, M.D.
Brian M. Gottlieb, M.D.
Daniel F. Hanley, M.D.
Peter J. Haughwout, M.D.
Gerry S. Hayes, M.D.
Mark F. Henry, M.D.
John H. Kanwit, M.D.
John T. Kennedy, Jr., M.D.
Ray N. Ketcham, M.D.
Augustus F. Kinzel, M.D.
Deryl P. Kipp, D.D.S.
Gerold K. V. Klein, M.D.
Myron K. Krueger, M.D.
C. Philip Lape, M.D.

Richard C. Leck, M.D.
Robert F. LeGendre, Jr., M.D.
Reuben Leitman, M.D.
Aldo F. Llorente, M.D.
Julia D. Lockwood, M.D.
Andrew M. Longley, D.O.
Lawrence J. Losey, M.D.
Charles F. Manning, Jr., M.D.
Henry L. McClintock, M.D.
Edward A. McFarland, M.D.
John F. McGeough, M.D.
Peter F. McGuire, M.D.
John J. McLaren, M.D.
David G. Millay, M.D.
Robert G. Mohlar, M.D.
Alain J. Montegut, M.D.
Douglas S. Most, D.D.S.
Robson S. Newbold, M.D.
Joseph R. O'Connor, M.D.
William Y. Oh, M.D.
Loren Olson, M.D.
Charles H. Patton, Jr., M.D.
David W. Schall, M.D.
Edward C. Schmidt, M.D.
Richard J. Seeley, M.D.
John C. Skillings, M.D.
Steven H. Stern, M.D.
Richard D. Stewart, M.D.
Geoffrey A. Stroud, M.D.
Ronald A. Swanson, M.D.
Donna K. Thompson, M.D.
Robert P. Timothy, M.D.
Raymond A. Tougas, M.D.
Wilhelm H. J. van Deventer, M.D.
Lloyd M. Van Lunen, Jr., M.D.
John S. Van Orden, M.D.
Michael L. Weaver, M.D.
M. W. Westermeyer, M.D.
Houghton M. White, M.D.
William G. Wilkoff, M.D.
Ralph E. Williams, M.D.
Rudolf G. Winkelbauer, M.D.
Elihu York, M.D.

REGIONAL MEMORIAL HOSPITAL
25TH ANNIVERSARY

6

A *new* DIRECTION

URING THE EARLY 1980s Bath Memorial Hospital was still experiencing financial difficulty. Trustees and management continued to see the need to compete with Regional. The Bath facility would require upgrading, modernizing, and developing a new wing. Bath Memorial went to the Maine Health and Higher Education Finance Authority seeking support to underwrite a bond issue, but what they learned was not encouraging. The hospital could not qualify to sell bonds through the Finance Authority due to its poor financial performance. A public community campaign raised $1,046,000 with Bath Iron Works contributing two dollars for every dollar donated. The board agreed to fund the remainder of the project out of equity capital, digging into the principal of the hospital's endowment for a total of $1.35 million. The project was developed and completed using these funds for a new emergency room, a new front entrance, new obstetrical facilities and additional areas for supporting services. The addition was aptly named the BIW Wing, and opened in 1984.

The initial opportunity for Bath and Regional to develop a cooperative effort came about in 1984. Following the unsuccessful efforts to develop a mutual approach for providing CT scanning services to the Bath-Brunswick area, Regional submitted a Certificate of Need application for a fixed base scanner to be located in its Brunswick facility. Once this application was submitted to the State Department of Human Services (DHS), it immediately precipitated two competing applications, from Bath and Parkview. The director of planning for the DHS indicated to all three hospitals that this was unacceptable and that no application would be entertained unless there was some effort to plan effectively for a single unit.

This announcement led to a series of discussions involving Bath, Parkview and Regional with radiologists, trustees and management representatives participating. After several meetings they reached a compromise with Bath agreeing to participate in a shared service with Regional for a fixed-based CT scanner located at Regional. The two hospitals would share equally in the acquisition costs. Parkview withdrew from those discussions, indicating that it did not wish to participate in this joint service, but agreed not to oppose the application for a fixed based unit and to support the service. Parkview's proposal for a mobile unit to travel among facilities did not go any further.

BATH IRON WORKS WING

Dedicated to the many
whose generous gifts made possible the
Bath Iron Works Wing at
Bath Memorial Hospital
July, 1984

A series of discussions ensued between the two hospitals leading to the development of a new corporation know as "Bath-Brunswick Shared Service Corporation." A new board drawn equally from representatives of Bath and Regional Hospitals was formed to oversee the new service. Following the installation, a dedication was held highlighting the working relationship of this new joint venture. Board members and medical staff representing the two hospitals worked harmoniously together in this cooperative effort.

Bath remained in a state of political turbulence and financial uncertainty even after these events. Physician relations problems began to surface and the financial woes of the hospital were making the situation very tenuous. The Bath board made a decision to dismiss Chief Executive Officer David Kelly and made a number of changes in the board, including electing new board leadership. The new chairperson Janet Bussey considered approaching Regional regarding a consolidation, but backed off in light of Bath's financial problems. A new administrator, Neil Bassett, was subsequently hired and quickly laid off a significant number of people which achieved temporary financial stability. Despite these changes, a fracture in community confidence remained. The hospital's census began to drop with many of its referrals going to Regional.

During this time Paris and Hodgdon approached the administration at Bath with the thought of trying to work together beyond the CT scanner project. Bassett was amenable to the idea and agreed to bring the subject to the planning committee of the board. It was also suggested that if there was interest on the part of the Bath board to enter into a dialogue with

Construction of the 1984
BIW *North wing at* BMH.

Regional then the invitation ought to come from the Bath board. A direct overture from the Regional board might hold the potential of being viewed as aggressive or threatening since Regional was the larger hospital and financially stable. At this point there was doubt that any kind of alliance could be formed between the two staunch competitors.

By December of 1985, the Bath planning committee was discussing the opportunity for joint planning with Regional, perceiving an environment threatened by future competition from larger hospitals and the appetites of national proprietary multi-hospital systems. The committee felt that quality of care could be further enhanced through working together as opposed to continuing the historical competition. Bath's planning committee followed up by inviting the Regional board to meet in January of 1986 to discuss joint planning possibilities. Members of this ad hoc group were drawn equally from the boards of directors, medical staff and management of the two hospitals. Their first meeting focused on what opportunities could be jointly pursued.

Discussion started slowly and awkwardly despite sufficient interest and trust that everyone would "check their hostilities at the door" to allow for a cordial environment. However, a level of trepidation clearly existed.

Initially discussions focused on new joint initiatives for collaboration by the two hospitals. After a couple of meetings the one idea that had been agreed upon was joint sponsorship of community Cardio Pulmonary Resuscitation training. While this was obviously a worthwhile idea, it was clear to everyone that it fell far short of the bolder step which would

be required to achieve meaningful change. At this point, the decision was made that an independent consultant should be retained to evaluate the opportunities and limitations of various consolidation models. The health consulting arm of Ernst and Young, a national accounting firm was engaged to help develop the agenda to facilitate further discussions. It was agreed that a careful and unbiased investigation of the two hospitals' financial structures, operations, endowments, strengths and weaknesses of the medical staff, management structures, and more would be explored.

A key event at this early stage was a private meeting between Paris, Regional CEO and Bassett, Bath CEO which focused on a frank discussion of personal goals and ambitions as they related to a potential merger. The goal of this meeting was to assure that the discussions were not encumbered by competitive attitudes for the leadership position. This discussion led to a tacit agreement that Paris would assume the position of Chief Executive Officer and Bassett would assume the role of Chief Operating Officer if the consolidation were to occur. This would prove to be a crucial catalytic force as the discussions grew and the process proceeded toward completion. Paris and Bassett understood that ultimately this would be a decision for the boards to make and that they would be free to make the decision to name an incumbent to these roles or to engage in a national search.

The joint planning committee went on to decide that there were a variety of joint venture possibilities, and that the possibilities would be researched over the course of several meetings with reporting back to their respective boards. The decision that began to emerge was that the most appropriate next stage would be to seek a consolidation of the two facilities, whereby each hospital would remain an independent, licensed entity, retaining its own board and medical staff, but create a parent board. The

1984 BMH BOARD OF TRUSTEES, FRONT *Mrs. Steven G. Buttner, Dr. William E. Howell, Dr. Robert S. Galen, Mrs. John F. Dougherty, Leonard C. Mulligan, President; Mrs. Lynn M. Bussey, First Vice President and Mrs. Lawrence G. Katz, Secretary* BACK *G. Baer Connard, Treasurer; David R. Flaherty, Raymond C. Small, Theodore K. Hoch, Esq., Harold D. Perry, Second Vice President; James E. Thorpe, Nicholas Sewall, and Mrs. Harry A Bishop, Jr. Absent when picture was taken are Edward D. True, II, Donald A. Spear, Esq., Colonel Joseph J. Rogers and Howard J. Yates.*

responsibilities of the parent board would be to provide a single management structure over the two facilities, consisting of a single finance committee, a single planning committee, and a single development committee, all made up of equal representation from the two facilities. The parent board would have the responsibility for the nominating process for future board membership of the two boards.

The approach would be that despite differences in financial conditions, operating scales and endowment funds, these two community hospitals, carrying out the full pride and ownership of their respective communities, should approach the process as equals coming together.

The management and boards of the hospitals realized that combining their talents would enhance both organizations and together the hospitals would be stronger than they would be by remaining competitors.

The joint planning committee also reached the conclusion that the full integration of the two organizations should be explored over and above looking at possible joint ventures. The planning committees for each hospital then reported back to their respective boards that they would begin to look toward the possibility of future affiliation and a potential merger. The concept of planning for the affiliation was approved with $50,000 marked for consultants and/or other experts who might be needed to facilitate planning efforts. A facilitator, William Caron of Ernst and Young, was engaged and the committee agreed to continue to meet on a regular and timely basis to outline what it wanted to accomplish, what type of corporate model might work and who should be involved.

A practical way needed to be found for the two competing hospitals to work cooperatively while preserving the familiar qualities of the individual community hospitals. In approaching this, representatives of the two hos-

Left: *Neil Bassett*
Right: *Herbert Paris*
1987.

pitals met with the Department of Human Services, which had licensing responsibilities, and the Maine Health Care Finance Commission. Regulators informally agreed that the possible affiliation was a sound move and offered their support and encouragement. The group began the process by asking the two hospital groups to independently develop their goals for the merger/consolidation, followed by what each organization perceived to be the advantages and disadvantages of merger/consolidation.

Goals for Bath Memorial Hospital included:

- Increase market penetration and broader service area boundaries.

- Strengthen the financial base to permit greater expansion and application of resources, i.e. greater access to capital, greater flexibility in negotiations (buying powers), and strong financial leverage.

- Create a corporate vehicle to facilitate diversification, expansion and acquisition of other competing and non-competing health care providers.

- Ensure against unwanted affiliations, takeovers, and other consuming pressures from parties external to the mid coast area.

- Provide for an expansion from primary to secondary levels of care.

- Allow for effective, productive and adaptive use of resources by both corporations.

- Provide services at a cost per unit less than other providers presently in this service area or other competitive forces which may enter the market.

Goals for Regional Memorial Hospital included:

- Broadening and strengthening the financial base of the hospital to become more competitive in the future.

- Improve access to obstetrical services as part of the overall organization.

- Increase marketshare.

- Achievement of greater economies of scale through cost containment and avoidance of duplication of services and personnel.

- Preserve the image of the hospital as a high quality institution and maintain a high level of confidence by the communities we serve.

Collectively the boards agreed on the advantages of such a merger/consolidation:

- Ensure long-term survival.

- Improved financial position resulting in increased negotiating power where leverage is strengthened and improved, economies of scale achieved and increased debt capacity occurring.

- Quality of care improved by providing for greater physician recruitment ability based on combined entity size, and improved clinical sophistication and technology in human resources. Combination of medical staffs result in broader based coverage, increased clinical interaction among practitioners, improved referral patterns and an increased basis for clinical knowledge and experience, all of which provide the necessary ingredients to move the organization from a primary care focus to a secondary level.

- Achieve and eventually excel in a secondary level of care not present in two local communities such as neurosurgery, expanded cardiology services, upgraded nursery services, dialysis, pulmonary intensive care specialists, infectious disease, etc.

- Increases in market coverage and penetration.

- Retain local controls.

- Add and expand upon the services unavailable in each individual facility, i.e. obstetrics at Regional and psychiatry at Bath.

- Provide for corporate diversification.

- Vertical integration of healthcare systems, i.e., acute chronic long-term rehabilitation, preventive community medicine and industrial medicine.

- Position for managed care alternatives.

- Institute competitive Health Maintenance Organization, Preferred Provider Organization plans.

The board recognized as disadvantages of a merger/consolidation:
- A perceived loss of autonomy by respective boards.

- Potential loss of employment and services as certain economies are instituted.

Members of the joint planning committee included: Janet Bussey, Katherine Buttner, Dr. Robert Dixon, Esther Dougherty, David Flaherty, Dr. Robert Galen, Nicholas Sewall, Theodore Yates and Neil Bassett, representing Bath; Horace Fay, Frank Goodwin, Dr. Gerry Hayes, Dr. Philip Lape, Richard Morrell, Campbell Niven, Edward Wilson, Lester Hodgdon and Herbert Paris representing Regional. The planning committee was augmented from time to time by outside consultants, legal expertise and financial expertise.

The joint planning committee agreed to collectively study four major aspects of each institution—thorough review of administrative, financial and medical staff and utilization profiles.

Also studied were personnel issues, organizational structure, benefits, general and professional liability issues, board composition, medical staff issues, financial and utilization data. Budget projections as well as the restricted funds for each hospital were reviewed and demographics were analyzed.

This thoughtful process began to reveal that there were no glaring differences in philosophy or practice between the two institutions. At this point the joint planning committee made a recommendation to the two respective boards that some form of consolidation be pursued. The boards were very responsive to this recommendation and asked the joint planning committee to proceed with the development of a model that would lead to either consolidation or merger of the two facilities.

This proved to be no easy task. The target was to combine the administrative and operational talents of two hospitals while enhancing both organizations and raising the quality of health care to the communities. The committee quickly found itself focused on defining an organizational model for consolidation, investigating a range of possibilities from simple affiliation to a full merger. The parent holding company model began to rise to the top as the most feasible because it allowed each hospital to retain its autonomy.

By January of 1987 the joint planning committee had worked out details of a plan of corporate affiliation, finalizing bylaws and amendments of the parent holding company corporate structure. The plan was to be presented to the Regional board, the Bath board, the two medical staffs and to the corporators for approval. In August of 1987 the Maine Health Care Finance Commission approved the consolidation of the two hospitals. The parent company, Mid Coast Health Services, was born as a not-for-profit corporation with two subsidiary organizations, Bath Memorial and Regional Memorial Hospitals. Herbert Paris was named president and chief executive officer of the new organization; Lester Hodgdon, chief financial officer; Neil Bassett, chief operating officer; and Lois Skillings, chief nursing officer.

More was needed to bringing two hospitals together than the legal, financial and regulatory issues. In the end social, engineering and organizational design equally shaped the process and defined its potential. It was an evolving process that took place over time and continued as the needs and talents of the people in the organization changed. As the process continued, the personal relationship that members of the two boards eventually built were critical to the understanding, discussions, and recommendations produced. The ability to work together as a group and the opportunity to socialize created the human network that forged the consolidation.

Immediately following consolidation, the staffs of both hospitals worked together within the framework of Mid Coast Health Services to resolve the differences and combine the decision-making processes while continuing to build and refine the organization, consolidate operations, and tighten finances.

The staffs also managed significant change. The change lived up to its reputation as an uncomfortable process. Bath and Regional had different cultures—culture defined as "the way things are done around here." All organizations have hundreds of unwritten rules and customs that govern behavior on the job, ranging from when you show up to work, to how you greet your fellow workers, from what you wear, to how seriously you approach your work.

The organizational values that employees live by are the core of any institutional culture. Hospital managers needed to build strong cultures into their own departments and then enforce them once they take hold. In this case, change meant creating (except where it made sense to operate separate departments such as plant maintenance and medical records) single departments between the two hospitals with single department managers to provide services to both hospitals with attention to quality and realistic budgets.

In order to allow change to occur smoothly, a period of grieving and transition was required. Grieving over "the way it used to be" took place over a period of many months. Course directions were continually assessed and minor changes made. Time was taken to carefully assess each situation and minimize surprises; in short, administration remained sensitive to the effects of change.

This sensitivity required a significant amount of "managing by wandering around," creating familiarity with the new management leadership team, seeking to build a rapport and understanding of issues and opportunities before any action was taken. Some of the practical issues that needed to be faced involved cross-training personnel, resistance to change, providing support and empathy for people resistant to change versus firing them, and the logistics of commuting between hospitals 10 miles apart. The change had a positive effect. The process itself was also a spark for creative problem solving. Policies and procedures were merged for the two facilities, and these new tools were stronger and better, reflecting the best thinking of both organizations.

Concurrent with the myriad operational, cultural, and organizational changes driven by the consolidation, the need to develop a clear vision for the growth and development of the whole system was apparent. To drive this vision various committees were established. One of the standing committees of the holding company was a corporate planning committee chaired by Mr. Campbell B. Niven, the owner and publisher of the *Times Record*, the local daily newspaper, located in Brunswick. Membership included board members, physicians and representatives from the senior management team.

Campbell B. Niven

A strategic plan needed to be developed for the system. The approach for developing the initial plan was thorough and comprehensive. The centerpiece was individual interviews with each member of the two medical staffs. In preparation for these interviews, a two-year profile of inpatient and outpatient activity was developed for each physician and used as a starting point for thinking about the future of each practice in terms of its relationship to the new system. Interviews were conducted by Herbert Paris and consultant Marc Voyvodich working as a team. As scientists, most physicians enjoyed reviewing the data and none had a very clear understanding of what their hospital utilization profile looked like in terms of a two-year trended analysis. While such data is more commonly available to physicians practicing in hospitals today, this was a new perspective in 1988, and proved an invaluable starting point for the medical staff members to think about the future.

Conversations were wide-ranging with discussions about future plans that each physician had for his or her practice, how Mid Coast Health Services could help strengthen practices, the need to recruit new physicians into the region, medical staff issues related and unrelated to the consolidation, hospital facility, and operational concerns. In many instances, this was the first chance for individual physicians to sit down with the chief executive officer and provide their opinions on where to go from here. Often these meetings were quite candid, and at times poignant, in terms of the personal concerns and fears that were divulged. From staffing problems, to marital concerns, to personality conflicts. These cathartic discussions helped to build strong new ties between physicians and management. In addition, a significant amount of trust building and information gathering occurred.

When the physician interviews were completed the strategic planning committee spent considerable time developing environmental assumptions regarding the future operating environment for the system. This included referral resources, payment systems, information technology, and outpatient care versus inpatient utilization. The committee reviewed extensive amounts of demographics, market share, volume, case mix, and

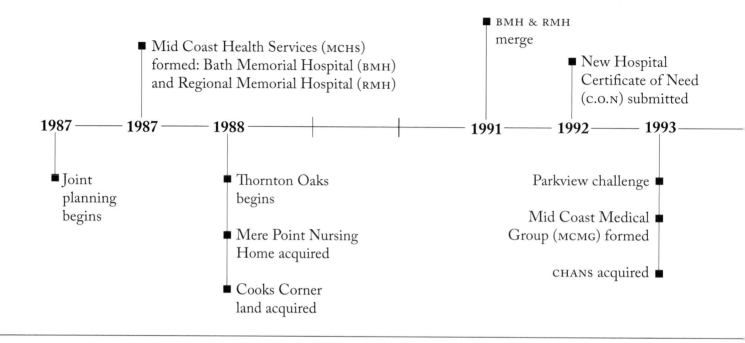

1987 —— 1987 —— 1988 ———— 1991 —— 1992 —— 1993 ——

Joint planning begins (1987)

Mid Coast Health Services (MCHS) formed: Bath Memorial Hospital (BMH) and Regional Memorial Hospital (RMH) (1987)

Thornton Oaks begins (1988)

Mere Point Nursing Home acquired (1988)

Cooks Corner land acquired (1988)

BMH & RMH merge (1991)

New Hospital Certificate of Need (C.O.N) submitted (1992)

Parkview challenge (1993)

Mid Coast Medical Group (MCMG) formed (1993)

CHANS acquired (1993)

other descriptive data. In a sense the committee was building a new statistical context and foundation for viewing the two hospitals as component parts of a larger consolidated system.

The committee also worked to develop a formal mission statement for the system. Drafts of the mission statement were developed by the senior management team. Varying drafts were reviewed by the committee.

Then a decision was made that a leadership group needed to offer the initial statement of mission. After all, thinking clearly about the mission and the role of the new systems was still an exercise in thinking "outside the box" of the independent hospital model, which had been abandoned only months before. The mission statement needed to anticipate such things as a new corporate subsidiary that had not even been conceptualized, new consolidated approaches to management, and potential new relationships with other healthcare organizations at a system level.

The statement which evolved out of these discussions was as follows:

> *"The Mission of Mid Coast Health Services shall be to work toward constantly improving the health and wellbeing of the people and the community it serves. It shall pursue this mission by supporting the humanistic, efficient, cost-conscious, convenient, and effective delivery of health care services by Regional Memorial Hospital, Bath Memorial Hospital and any other health service corporation which it may come to own, manage, or affiliate.*

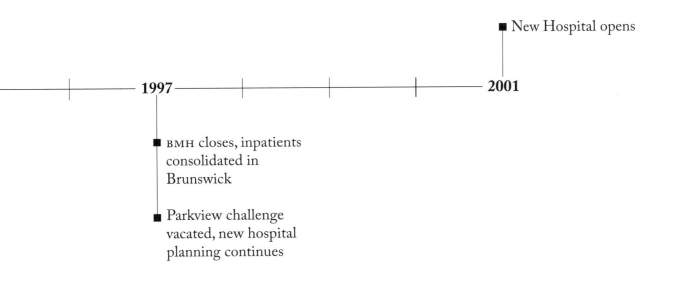

■ New Hospital opens

1997 ——————————————— 2001

■ BMH closes, inpatients
consolidated in
Brunswick

■ Parkview challenge
vacated, new hospital
planning continues

*The administrative support shall include management services;
strategic and financial planning services; public information and
fundraising; professional, patient, and community health education services; liaison with other healthcare organizations; and
other efforts which the board may determine are consistent with
improving the health and wellbeing of the population in the communities served."*

The creation of Mid Coast Health Services was initiated by a desire to
establish a successful organizational model that would facilitate economies of scale, a broader mix of locally accessible medical specialty services,
more complete and integrated continuum of locally available health and
social services and access to the best medical and hospital staff available. The powerful external economic forces, such as the rise of managed
care and Medicare reimbursement, created unprecedented pressures on
community hospitals throughout Maine and the nation to provide more
efficient and higher quality services. The creation of Mid Coast Health
Services represented a timely response to these forces.

In the first year of these efforts, $300,000 in reduced expenditures was
achieved, as well as another $250,000 in savings realized as a result of the
consolidation.

The early success of the new organizational structure gave further valid-
ity to the vision that at some future time one facility, centrally located,

In 1989, the committee
looking into the
acquisition of land for
a new hospital was
determined to find a
location equidistant
between Bath and
Brunswick.

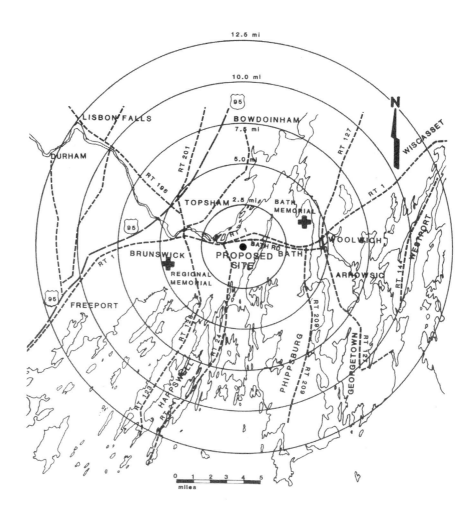

might better serve the area's health care needs. A single facility would
attract and support a greater base of physicians and specialty services, and
eliminate the need for patient travel out of the area for those services. In
addition, one facility would maximize the skills of healthcare professionals,
be more efficient and economical, and eliminate the need to duplicate expensive technology. As part of the long-range planning process, the board
had determined that it was both prudent and timely to purchase land for
a possible future facility. Further, if the decision to acquire land was not
made, then it was unlikely that such land would be available in the future
or if it were available, it would be at a price that the hospitals could not
afford.

To this end, a small committee of board members under the leadership
of Richard A. Morrell and including David Flaherty, Campbell B. Niven,
John G. Morse, Jr. and Herbert Paris was formed to look into the possibility of acquiring land. City and town maps were spread over the conference table in Paris's office and they looked at areas equidistant from Bath

Richard A. Morrell

and Brunswick. A large area just east of Cook's Corner had a number of contiguous lots which were unused. Each committee member was assigned a lot in an attempt to meet with the owners and propose an option for one year to purchase the land. Clearly the members of the committee would disclose to the owners the idea of a new hospital to be built in the future. About 150 acres were available on the contiguous lots and the committee was successful in acquiring options from Joseph Footer for 43 acres, from the Conover Family Limited Partnership 41.4 acres, from the Brunswick Shopping Plaza Trust 15.5 acres and from C. Warren Ring about 50 acres. Subsequently, Ring donated an additional 18 acres to the hospital some 10 years later.

With these options in hand the committee felt that it had sufficient acreage to develop a broad range of healthcare services and facilities in the future. Central to the hospital's service area, this land was easily accessible from both communities as well as Route 1. Cost of the land, fees, survey studies and other contingencies related to the acquisition would be $850,000. Hospital leadership hoped and desired to raise these funds in the communities in gifts and pledges payable over a three-year period. Once the land was purchased the board of directors was committed to a continuing and orderly process of planning for the new hospital complex. Included in the process would be the establishment of a clear strategy for how the existing facilities and campuses of Regional and Bath could be utilized.

It was again clear to all that a successful fundraising campaign would be a strong endorsement and validate this strategy of a long-range vision of a single hospital serving the area. The campaign was undertaken by John G. Morse, Jr. and successfully raised $850,000 in a matter of several months. The purchases of the land were completed and owned by Mid Coast Health Services in 1989.

John G. Morse, Jr.

As the planning process proceeded, specific recommendations were generated, which were taken in draft form to a special meeting of the entire medical staff for comments. This evening meeting was punctuated by several impassioned monologues by physicians regarding the impending demise of the hospitals due to the development of managed care systems. Some of these physicians were members of the board of a newly formed, physician owned, Health Maintenance Organization named HealthSource and were using the meeting as a platform for attracting new recruits.

Despite this distraction, physicians did not take issue with the recommendations presented, in large part because they each had an opportunity for individual input and viewed the recommendations as a reflection of their collective thinking.

Vice President for Finance Lester Hodgdon, seated, reviews details of the merger with Vice President for Operations Philip Ortolani.

THE MERGER

The creation of Mid Coast Health Services in August of 1987 was initiated by a desire to establish a successful organizational model that would facilitate economies of scale, a broader mix of locally accessible medical specialty services, a more complete and integrated continuum of locally available health and social services, and access to the best medical and hospital staffs available. With the operational success of the consolidation of the hospitals, the communities had the benefit of enhanced patient care technologies, while at the same time controlling health care costs. With nuclear medicine capabilities in Bath and CT scanning capabilities at Regional, each hospital was able to offer these services to patients without duplicating equipment. Concurrent with the operational success was the growing comfort through the socialization process of the boards of trustees of the two hospitals. Repeated opportunities for social gatherings and meetings at which substantial issues were discussed, a growing sense of mutual trust and admiration for the commitment and goals of each group began to build. The consolidation of the finance, development, planning, and personnel committees allowed for the philosophy of the individual trustees to be discussed with the realization that both groups aspired to the same goals. In a meeting of the joint medical staff executive committee, determination was made that it would be mutually beneficial to begin cooperative efforts toward the combining of the two medical staffs. Common bylaws and credentialing procedures needed to be addressed early in the process. A combined Bath/Regional joint conference committee, composed of members of the two medical staffs, both boards, and representatives of administration, was requested to begin discussions regarding the merger of the medical staffs.

At the Mid Coast Health Services board meeting on October 16, 1989, directors unanimously agreed to appoint a special task force to complete the merger of the two hospitals. This would have the effect of co-mingling assets and liabilities of the two institutions and include the combining of the two hospital boards into the Mid Coast Health Services board. This special task force would address the financial, regulatory, medical staff, legal, organizational and governance issues. Appointed by Richard A. Morrell, board chairman of Mid Coast Health Services, the task force included representatives of the Mid Coast Health Services board, the Bath and Regional boards, and the medical staffs. The task force met monthly with progress reports made to the boards, medical staffs, finance and long range planning committees as appropriate. An interim progress report was made to the corporators at their annual meeting January 13, 1991. A final report was available in April of 1991 with recommendations made to the boards of directors, medical staff and corporators for approval in late spring of 1991. Ernst and Young was again retained as consultants, and supported by the management staff.

Janet B. Bussey

It was clear that the board of Mid Coast Health Services had from the outset devoted a great deal of time and energy to a careful study of future needs and how best to meet them. This effort resulted in a thoughtfully constructed, long range plan approved by the two hospital boards as well as Mid Coast Health Services. The merger of all the elements of Bath and Regional hospitals into a single entity was an important step toward the goal of establishing a single hospital to serve the southern mid coast area in an effective and efficient manner, and would affect a significant change in our capabilities to provide high quality health care services.

In the fall of 1991 the board of Mid Coast Health Services saw that it would be beneficial to begin the merger. Morrell said, "We would gain immeasurably from increased efficiencies, coordinated health care delivery, improved quality of care and a potential for further improving the financial health of Mid Coast Health Services as a whole."

Richard A. Morrell, Chairman of the Board, and Herbert Paris, President of Mid Coast Health Services, display the hospitals' new name.

Regional Memorial Hospital was merged into the Bath Memorial Hospital with the name of the remaining corporation changed to Mid Coast Hospital effective October 1, 1991.

Over the previous three years great leadership was shown by Janet B. Bussey, President of the Bath board. She recognized the benefits to be gained by the merger, and enthusiastically endorsed the effort as did the other board members.

7

PLANNING
for the FUTURE

As the momentum for the new hospital planning effort began to build, so did the recognition that the planning effort had to reach far beyond the question of facility design. The facility had to anticipate and accommodate the likelihood for changes in medical technology, delivery system standards, and payment systems; all were likely to be greater in the coming several decades than had already been observed through the rear view mirror.

After considerable debate and discussion by both the management team and the strategic planning committee, eight specific focuses for the planning process were identified. These were graphically summarized by a circle with eight wedges that was labeled, "The Planning Pie."

THE TEAM

The direction of Mid Coast Health Services was set by the board of directors led by Chairman Richard A. Morrell and Herbert Paris, President and Chief Executive Officer of MCHS. The senior management team included Lester Hodgdon, Chief Financial Officer; Robert McCue, Controller; Lois Skillings, Vice President for Nursing and Patient Care Services; George Hunter, Vice President for Human Resources and Administration, Philip Ortolani, Vice President for Operations, and Dr. Scott Mills represented the medical staff leadership. Marc Voyvodich served as a consultant. Campbell B. Niven chaired the Planning Committee of the Board of Trustees.

Following the consolidation of the two hospitals, efforts began to turn toward the development of a single hospital. It became obvious that this could not be done as an isolated element in the delivery of healthcare by the Mid Coast Health Services organization. Rapid changes were taking place in technology, in the financing of healthcare, and in the overall provision of healthcare services. In viewing the complexities that faced the hospital and the overall vision that we had developed for the Mid Coast Health Services, the future of the planning efforts had to include a number of elements which ultimately had to be integrated. The "planning pie" emerged and included these pieces: 1) planning for the hospital merger; 2) an information system; 3) interface with purchasers and payors; 4) development of a support service program; 5) clinical services that included entrepreneurial planning; 6) physician/hospital relations; 7) interface with other community providers; and 8) campus/facility planning.

Completion of the merger in 1991 resulted in a successful consolidation of the two acute hospitals into a single licensed provider with a single board, medical staff, budget, and a set of financial requirements.

The next element to be addressed was the hospital-wide information system. The goal of this effort was to develop a technology plan which identified future clinical, operational, management, corporate planning, physician networking, and other requirements. The plan included defining hardware, software, and timeframe requirements.

The interface planning with purchasers and payors had the goal to develop an ongoing process of establishing preferred relationships with

Left to right: Lester Hodgdon, Chief Financial Officer; Robert McCue, Controller; Philip Ortolani, Vice President for Operations; Herbert Paris, President and Chief Executive Officer; Lois Skillings, Vice President for Nursing and Patient Care Services; George Hunter, Vice President for Human Resources and Administration.

key employers and third party payors. The intended results would be to encourage, through financial and other incentives, employees, patients, and physicians to use Mid Coast Hospital.

In planning for support services, the goal was to develop plans through an entrepreneurial process which defined each support service in sufficient detail that could be interpreted into a space program, capital requirement needs, and the new facility design. This planning would sequentially follow the clinical services planning effort.

In planning for clinical services, department directors were encouraged to think in new and different ways about community needs, and to be entrepreneurial by developing new models for volume, revenue, staff, space, and equipment. This information could then be used to develop a space program, equipment needs and an effective design for the new hospital.

In planning for physician/hospital relations, the goal was to develop a plan that defined future directions in terms of the organization, business, and campus/facility relationships between Mid Coast Health Services and groups of physicians. The plan needed to project as specifically as possible the scope and scale of primary care and specialty services to be located within the hospital complex.

The goal of planning with other community providers for an effective interface was to identify clinical and operational alliances with other hospitals and community based health providers in the region. Relationships of special interest included Maine Medical Center in Portland, Parkview Memorial Hospital, Community Health and Nursing Services (CHANS home health agency), and Shoreline Mental Health Services (the community mental health system).

The final element was planning for the new campus/facility. Here the goal was a three-phased planning process to include: 1) a site development and campus plan; 2) a functional program that defined service, sizing, and adjacencies; and 3) a facility design. This process would also include development of a Certificate of Need and other applications requiring necessary regulatory approvals.

Thus we set out an overall design and planning structure which would ultimately lead to a new facility whose components were integrated among all elements of service delivery, while at the same time meeting the needs of the community and providing effective working relationships with other healthcare providers in the community.

RECIPE FOR A NEW DELIVERY SYSTEM
In order to fully explore the opportunities in front of Mid Coast Health Services with regard to planning for the future, an application for a two-

year funding grant was made to the Bingham Foundation in Boston. The purpose of this grant request was to study the issues and prepare recommendations for the future directions of Mid Coast Health Services. With the aid of Voyvodich and Dr. Daniel Hanley, a board member of the Bingham Foundation, a $150,000 grant was approved and served as the foundation for the planning efforts going forward.

The joint planning committee agreed that the development of a new campus and facility without simultaneously considering the other wedges of the pie would be naïve. Regardless of the outcome regarding the building of a new hospital, the merits of merging the two existing subsidiaries into a single hospital corporation was becoming apparent. While this entailed a number of regulatory, legal, financial, and other technical issues, the biggest issue by far was the political task of turning two medical staffs into one. The new Mid Coast Hospital looked and operated pretty much the same on October 1, 1991 as it had the day before. However, its creation was a powerful symbol of progress toward a better integrated delivery system for the region. What was two had become one.

While there was reliance on structural engineering services in the design of a new hospital, perhaps the most important type of engineering required was in the social arena. Much progress had been made since the consolidation of Bath and Regional into Mid Coast Health Services in 1987. However, there was still no community consensus for pursuing the integrated delivery system dream. One major problem was that relatively few people in the hospital or in the community truly comprehended why there was a need to disturb the status quo.

The solution to this was educating the community. The internal planners, lead by Paris, Hodgdon and Voyvodich, decided that some of the grant funds should be used to create a seminar series, designed to provide all members of the Mid Coast community with a fuller understanding of the forces shaping the future of health care. The *Mid Coast Health Services 2000* symposium was an effort to try to understand where Mid Coast Health Services might be in the next decade.

The series of eight seminars were offered free to Mid Coast Health Services board, medical staff, senior managers, department directors, corporators, area business people and community residents. Continuing education credits were available to physicians and nurses. The seminars were held at Bowdoin College and outstanding national speakers were invited to present their vision of the future of healthcare.

The series began in March of 1991 with a presentation by Jerome Grossman MD, the president of the New England Medical Center and executive director of the Bingham Program. This set the stage for a series

Marc Voyvodich, planning consultant

Lester Hodgdon, Chief Financial Officer 1979–2004

that continued through the following year with a variety of issues presented and debated, including: continuous quality improvement in the hospital environment, the role of information systems in community hospitals and local delivery systems, physician/hospital linkages and the respective roles of regulation and competition, the integration of medical practice and hospital design, and the economics of health care delivery.

As the months went by, the cumulative impact of these seminars became evident. It would have been impractical to take the entire staff beyond the cloistered hospital environment to visit organizations further along the evolutionary path of integrated systems development, but bringing experts from other organizations to Mid Coast did prove both practical and effective. Despite this influx of expertise and experience, almost every speaker shared one fundamental theme he or she did not have the final model or answer. Best summed up by futurist Russell Coile, who said "Your future is going to be uniquely local. It's going to reflect the warmth, the needs, the values, the attitudes, the expectations, and the resources of the people here, and while you may be inspired and illuminated by some of the things that are going on in other places, those things are going to play out differently here than they would in other parts of the country, and that's appropriate. You get to shape, you get to manage, you get to influence your own future and that's how it should be."

ENTREPRENEURIAL PROGRAM PLANNING

As the preliminary planning for the new hospital began to take on a reality and life of its own, Hodgdon became increasingly concerned about the potential for managers and department directors to develop unrealistic expectations about the space they would be allocated in the new hospital. His concern was that mid-level managers would view the new hospital planning process as an isolated event unrelated to the need to increase efficiency, to generate revenue, to reach out into the community, and to offer medical and health services products responsive to community need, and to be well positioned in an increasingly price competitive environment. A response to this concern emerged labeled 'Entrepreneurial Planning.' The purpose of entrepreneurial planning was to guide and to motivate mid level managers to think in a strategic, long-range fashion. With the Mid Coast 2000 seminars as context they would be challenged to think beyond the traditional annual operational planning boundaries for their departments, and to develop "business plans" that addressed specific factors:

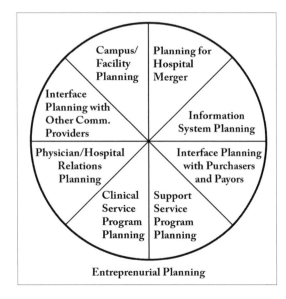

current products, customers, competitors, current operating volume and long range trends, staffing needs, factors indicating future community service and affiliations, alliances and relationships within and outside the hospital.

As this process went into high gear in the summer of 1991 it was augmented and facilitated by the recruitment of a full-time planning staff member, Richard Linehan, whose position was partially funded by the Bingham Foundation. Linehan organized department user groups, developed templates to organize the data, and encouraged cross fertilization of thinking among the groups.

As the mid-level planning process evolved, the CFO Hodgdon continued to express cautionary concerns. Significant amounts of time were being invested in the effort. Some directors were responding to the challenge of productivity and vision, while others were intimidated by the new territory into which they were thrust. As the volume projections, staffing patterns, and new services expectations were converted into preliminary space projections, Hodgdon's concerns were realized. Initial space expectations were nearly 75% over its target.

WHAT WENT WRONG?

In retrospect it appeared that unrealistic expectations were placed upon middle management. Like similar initiatives in other organizations aimed at creating product line management structures, or continuous quality improvement systems, success is very dependent upon a major commitment to development of new skill sets, new paradigms, new information, support and structures, and ultimately change in organizational culture.

The entrepreneurial planning process tried to challenge middle managers to think and to plan for the future of their departments in new and ambitious ways. The process failed to give them the skill base and tools, which would enable such growth to be successful.

This is not to say that the entrepreneurial planning process was a complete failure. Creative new ideas were born. The best thinking was gathered and reflected in new near term operational directions, as well as plans for the new hospital. The appetite for the revolution in management at Mid Coast was part of W. Edward Deming's plans for revolutionizing manufacturing in Japan and the United States. This philosophy was brought to the management team by Ortolani, Vice President for Operations. While neither Mid Coast nor Deming's dreams had been fully realized, Mid Coast did get a respectable return on an admittedly inadequate level of investment in revolutionizing its management approach.

As the vision of an integrated delivery system was scrutinized in greater detail, the importance of information systems planning climbed to the top of the priority list. The importance was amplified because the license for Mid Coast's existing information systems software was scheduled to expire the end of 1991. A long-range information systems plan needed to be developed even though Mid Coast's capacity for planning its future was already being tested.

To ease this burden, a medical information systems consultant was retained to lead the process, which began with educational sessions. Reviewed were the state-of-the-art hospital information technology presented as part of *Mid Coast Health Services 2000* series. Specific needs and the ability of various vendors to address them were explored. A needs assessment focused on physicians, department directors and other information system users, augmented by direct interviews with directors and physicians.

The most controversial issue to emerge was predictable. Does it make sense to change medical information system vendors given the cost and complexity of a system conversion? Should we keep a system that offered superior features in specific areas such as laboratory, even though interface with the hospital-wide system may be problematic? Should vendors with superior systems and support be considered even if they have a relatively small installed base and their long-term staying power may be questionable? In the end, a field of 30 potential vendors was narrowed down to two with the final decision going to the incumbent company. All major applications would be assessed through this vendor to ensure ease of integration.

NEW DIRECTIONS

A variety of major new directions emerged from the initial strategic planning and guided the activities of Mid Coast Hospital into the 1990s.

A forum was created to think through in greater detail the future course that Mid Coast Health Services would need to take in order to bring together the hospital and medical staff. Named the physician/hospital interface committee, it became the centerpiece of a plan that would produce recommendations to recruit 14 new physicians. The new practices would be distributed among a variety of primary care and medical/surgical sub-specialties, representing a controversial increase of over 10% in the number of physicians in the area. Physician recruitment was not an initiative that had garnered much support from members of either hospital's medical staff. However, since the recommendations were based upon data,

2003 GASTROENTEROLOGY GROUP
Richard Beveridge MD *and John Bosco* MD

2003 ULTRASOUND GROUP: FRONT *Jean Lehman, Carmen Footer and Kim Ziegler* BACK *Ellen Denson, Corey Stainer and Mitsy Stainer*

2005 ANESTHESIOLOGY GROUP: FRONT *Wendy Love* MD *and Todd Clow* DO, MIDDLE *Irl L. Rosner* MD *and Andrew Rabinowitz* MD, BACK *Sean L. Kelly* MD

2005 DIAGNOSTIC IMAGING: *Sue Borge, Mark Legasse, Jan McGoin, and Cheryl Kennedy*

2005 OBGYN NURSES. FRONT *Penny Hauser, Janet Burns, Eileen Delaney and Kelly Gordon* MIDDLE *Amy Aieta, Jane Lang, Peggy Martin, Fay Beaudoin, Jessica Berube, Kathy Recknagel, Mary Wallace, Patty Chubbuck, Jody Kaufman, Rhiannon Hughes, Sue Dentico, Wendy O'Connor Linda Jeffers, Jeri Walker and Ellen Wanser* BACK *Kristi Yancey, Rachel Gallagher, Claire Vachon, Melissa Palmer, Charlene Wyman and Kathy Rose*

2005 LABORATORY GROUP: FRONT *Christie Robert, Jane Sarazin, Claudia Eckert, Sujiata Mukhopadyhay* MD *and Michelle Nickles* SECOND *Lisa Lavesseur, Gina Perow and Vicki Mignaull* THIRD *Sue Ross, Roy Defio, and Linda Hodgkins* BACK *Gail Mulrooney, Charlene Fox, and Pat Fortier.*

coupled with significant medical staff input, the recruitment target was not contested.

Part of this thinking was a possible initiative by Mid Coast Hospital to develop a primary care group practice. The recruitment of physicians into solo practices was becoming significantly more challenging and the ability to provide continuous medical care for the community was at risk.

After much debate and discussion the physician/hospital interface committee decided to recommend that a hospital-based group (Mid Coast Medical Group) be created as a separate corporate entity under the holding company. This recommendation was brought to a special meeting of the full medical staff at a Sunday morning meeting and attended by a majority of the active medical staff. The recommendation was vigorously debated, with camps arguing for an independent, market-driven solution to be developed independently by medical staff members, or for a Mid Coast based approach grounded more deeply in the metrics of community need rather than a business opportunity. In the end both directions ended up being pursued.

Mid Coast's role was complicated by a subsequent independent initiative by a group of primary care physicians led by Dr. David Schall of the Regional staff to create their own organization. About 12 physicians, ultimately known as Bowdoin Medical Group, formed a cooperative, hired staff, obtained bank financing, and embarked on an aggressive development effort that was at times confrontational.

The Bowdoin Medical Group was created during the same period as the establishment of Mid Coast Medical Group. Both were occurring at the same time that managed care contracting initiatives were starting to have a significant impact on the Bath/Brunswick market.

The relationship between Mid Coast Hospital and the Bowdoin Medical Group was complex. First, Bowdoin Medical Group decided to build a substantial medical facility. The options were to locate it adjacent to the existing Mid Coast Hospital property in Brunswick (formally known as Regional Memorial Hospital on Baribeau Drive) or to become the first development on the campus being planned for the new hospital. The uncertainty of the political and regulatory issues confronting Mid Coast Hospital at the time ended up pushing Bowdoin Medical Group to a decision to locate next to the existing facility. The Bowdoin Medical Group, as a struggling new business, looked to the hospital for help, particularly in terms of an opportunity to assume responsibility for the physician emergency room contract. Mid Coast Hospital decided to take an inclusive approach in working with all physicians on the medical staff. Therefore, a decision was made to contract with the Bowdoin Medical

2013 NEUROLOGY
GROUP, TOP TO
BOTTOM: *John A.
Taylor* DO, *William P.
Stamey* MD, *Kathryn D.
Seasholtz* DO.

Group for these services, even though there was an understanding at the time that this was "promoting the competition."

Soon the Bowdoin Medical Group decided to directly compete with the hospital in diagnostic services, including both laboratory and radiology. However the duality of the relationship was such that the Bowdoin Medical Group subsequently contracted radiology services back to the hospital. A conundrum that many hospitals experience is the necessity of working with doctors who are simultaneously partners and competitors. Mid Coast Hospital's challenge was to continue to look at the need from a community versus a business perspective, and to understand that if the new hospital was to emerge, it would necessarily be built on a foundation of a dynamic set of relationships where the physicians and the hospital would continue as both competitors and collaborators. Required were innovation, vision, responsiveness, and some level of chutzpah. In 2009, after a decade of operations, the Bowdoin Medical Group was absorbed into Martin's Point Health Care, a Portland based managed care organization.

The formation of Mid Coast Medical Group was necessitated in part by the realization that physicians from the Bath community were beginning either to retire or to move to other communities. Bath physicians in particular had not had any group practice development and thus there was no structure to recruit new or replacement physicians into the Bath community.

The Mid Coast Medical Group started with the financial support and backing of Mid Coast Health Services. This was particularly irksome to Brunswick primary care physicians, who argued that the hospital was moving tax exempt resources into the Bath community that could end up competing with them unfairly. This conflict was highlighted sharply when the Bowdoin Medical Group threatened to file suit against Mid Coast after Mid Coast expressed intent to recruit a primary care physician into Topsham. Bowdoin Medical Group already had eyes on this community as a growth option for its practice, but was pre-empted by Mid Coast Medical Group. The ongoing friction between perception of community need and competitive threat was impossible to avoid when the interest of physicians and hospitals were not fully aligned. In the midst of these primary care debates, another key priority needed attention: the consolidation of the Bath and Brunswick medical staffs. While the two hospitals had been operationally consolidated through an integrated management structure, the two medical staffs remained independent. The importance of bringing them together for credentialing, quality assurance, utilization management, and planning was apparent but not palatable for many.

Medical staff integration was delayed at the time of the merger as a

2006 MID COAST MEDICAL GROUP: FRONT *Carl S. DeMars* MD, *Catharine M. Cadigan* MD *and Nancy A. Hassenfus* MD, BACK *Benjamin S. Herman* MD, *James P. Rines* MD, *Scott N. French* MD, *Daniel Wood* MD *and Matthew T. Hanna* MD

2007 SURGICAL GROUP: FRONT *Ira Bird* MD *and Nathaniel W. Hyde* MD, BACK *William Curtis* MD *and Gregory A. Kelly* MD

2008 PULMONARY/CRITICAL CARE AND SLEEP MEDICINE: FRONT *Abbey France and Mary Jo Weatherbee* RN, MIDDLE *Hal I. Sreden* MD *and Paul J. LaPrad* MD, BACK *Laura Coghlin, Patrick J.Keaney* MD *and James McCormick* MD

2009 RUNNING START, CARDIAC & PULMONARY REHABILITATION, FRONT *Margo Kovach* RN *and Celeste Pascarella* RN, BACK *Sharon Miller* RN, *Keith Guiou* MS *and Mark Cushman* RT

2009 COASTAL ORTHOPEDICS, FRONT *Laura Smith-Tucker* FNP *and Carmen Blackstone* FNP, BACK *Robert Livingston* MD, *Mark Henry* MD, *John Van Orden* MD *and Stephen Katz* MD

2010 MID COAST SUBSTANCE ABUSE PREVENTION PROGRAM / ACCESS HEALTH, FRONT *Terry Goan, Lois Skillings, Amanda Hopkins, Jaki Ellis and Melissa Fochesato* MIDDLE *Andrea Nicoletta, Heidi Tucker, Rebecca Farnham and Geno Ring,* BACK *Michael Field, Terry Sherman, Mary Booth and Pat Conner*

CARING FOR OUR COMMUNITIES

practical matter—an issue of timing and comfort, but there was an understanding that ultimately this would be a *fait accompli*. There was little advantage of pushing this to closure when time was needed to build rapport among the two staffs.

The medical staff merger ultimately occurred within two years of the merger with some sense of enthusiasm.

Over time it has become a trend for physicians to seek opportunities in hospital based practices. By the end of 2010 the Mid Coast Medical Group had grown to 70 physicians. As Mid Coast Hospital continued to be active in the recruitment of physicians, the Mid Coast Medical Group grew into a multi-specialty group practice. Primary care physician practices are located in Bath, Brunswick and Topsham, and the specialists tend to cluster on the main campus close to the hospital. Indeed the growth of the Mid Coast Medical Group practice reflects the changing needs of the medical community and its sub-specialty practices. Maine Medical Center, with its extensive specialty and sub-specialty practices, well established, and only 26 miles from Brunswick, provides a close clinical affiliation already in place with Mid Coast Hospital.

LONG TERM CARE

Another priority identified in the strategic plan was to establish a focus on long term care. The plan presented the concept of developing a full spectrum of services for the aging population including the acquisition of Mere Point Nursing Home in 1990 and the development of a retirement community on the Brunswick campus, Thornton Oaks Retirement Community is comprised of 46 private homes and 100 apartments on 29 acres located adjacent to the former RMH. It was completed in 2003.

Creating other programs that would fill out a service continuum, included assisted living, respite care, hospice, dementia care, elderly day care, geriatric assessment and home care. Several factors were driving this emerging agenda. One was an aging population. Acute care would not be a sufficient focus alone for an organization like MCHS that described its mission as including preserving and improving health status. A second factor was the political and business imperative associated with the alternative programming to utilize one or both of the existing hospital facilities. The investment in these facilities would not simply disappear with the development of a new hospital. Extracting future value from the existing bricks and mortar was a challenge that could not be ignored in the long run.

There was recognition by management that the hospital had to evolve from the free-standing care concept to a continuum of care spec-

2014 PSYCHIATRY GROUP, TOP *Brian Viele* RN, *Director of Inpatient Behavioral Health* MIDDLE *Tatyana Karchov* MD, *Chief of Psychiatry* BOTTOM *Jeffrey Stenzel* MD, *Medical Director of Behavioral Health.*

trum—from prevention, to primary care, to acute care services, to rehabilitative and long term care, and to home and hospice care. Mid Coast's vision was to vertically integrate the system to effectively coordinate and leverage each of these elements of patient care. This vision continued to shape the direction and priorities of MCHS as it prepared itself for the next century.

The final major priority within the strategic plan was to launch an effort to develop a new inpatient facility which would replace the two existing sites. This recommendation was still an extremely controversial idea and was cautiously approached. The language used emphasized that the initial planning efforts were not to be construed as a commitment on the part of the system to implement these plans without careful analysis and specific recommendations.

In retrospect, this initial foray into strategic planning at the system level identified the major themes and directions which continued to direct Mid Coast as it entered the mid 1990s. The process itself was carefully customized to deal with the specific circumstances of identifying and meeting community needs, and influenced by the political sensitivities of the moment, but not dominated by them. In short, the process legitimized and endorsed an agenda for ambitious growth and development into the future.

2010 PEDIATRIC SURGICAL NURSING GROUP, FRONT *Lynne Pinkham, Carol Wartz, Phyllis Smith, Sue Matzell, Estelle Krestos and Karen Drew* BACK *Susan Davis, Kim Hunter, Susan Novak, Renee Powers, Leean Sargent, Deb Cote and Bettie Kettell*

2010 MIDCOAST EYE ASSOCIATES, FRONT *Gregory Gensheimer* MD *and Marybeth Ford* MD BACK *Kurt Kelly* MD *and Mark Moratto* MD

2011 CARDIOLOGY GROUP, FRONT *R. Scott Schafer* MD *and Ellen M. Simon* MD, BACK *Benjamin A. Lowenstien* MD, *Paul R. Burns* MD *and Scott D. Mills* MD

2012 WOMEN'S HEALTH GROUP, *left to right: Stephanie Holmes* FNP, *Cathy Houston* FNP, *Melissa Streeter* MD, *Elaine Sesckas* MD, *Gregory Gimbel* MD, *Stephanie Grohs* MD, *Lisa Moratto* MD, *Darcey Leighton* DO, *Suzi Zimmerman* CNM, *Natalie Rockwell* CNM *and Angela Ripley* CNM

2012 WOUND CARE & PODIATRY, FRONT *Patsy Cyr* FNP, MIDDLE *Jasmin Satchwell* CNA *and Mary Beth Maclean,* BACK *Lisa Gatti* CNA *and Angela Perron* DPM

2014 MIDCOAST UROLOGY GROUP, *Michael R. Curtis* MD, *Amy. B. Bosinske* PA-C, *Francine D'Alfonso* FNP *and Craig A. Hawkins* MD

2014 NURSE LEADERS FRONT *Sue Lewis* RN, *Lynne Pinkham* RN, *Pat Miller, Deb McLeod* RN, *Barb McCue* RN, *Carolyn Koepke* RN, *Liz Mann* RN *and Christine Hanson* RN, BACK *Eileen Delaney* RN, *Rosemary Cummings* RN, *Paul Parker* RN, *Lauren Doran* RN, *Brian Viele* RN, *Matt Hincks* RN *and Cindy Metivier. Absent when picture was taken: Lori Allen* RN, *Vicky Koehler* RN, *and Cate Parker* RN.

8

Beyond Acute Care:
FORGING *a* COMMUNITY
DELIVERY SYSTEM

Tʜᴇ ᴠɪsɪᴏɴ of Thornton Oaks began with the strategic plan of Regional Memorial Hospital in 1983. With the arrival of Paris in 1978
the immediate needs of Regional were addressed with the 1982 edition
providing a new emergency room, new operating room facilities and a
general remodeling of the support services of the hospital. It was not until
1983 that the hospital board and management team turned their attention
to developing a strategic plan which envisioned a community hospital
organization that extended beyond the acute care hospital and that could
provide a continuum of care including an independent retirement community, assisted living, long term care, dementia care, home care, respite
care and rehabilitative services and physician practices.

The retirement community concept emerged concurrently with the
formation of Mid Coast Health Services (ᴍᴄʜs). In 1985 the Thornton
Oaks Development Corporation was formed as a separate for-profit
corporation with the specific assignment of researching the feasibility of
developing a retirement community. A recommendation was presented to
the ᴍᴄʜs Board in the strategic plan of 1986. This concept was embraced
by the board which authorized management to continue the development of such a project. Millie Stewart, Director of Volunteers of Regional
Memorial Hospital, suggested the name of Matthew Thornton, a one
time resident whose family lived on the Rossmore Road in the 1700s. The

Thornton Oaks

family lived in Brunswick for a relatively short period of time before being forced to leave by the Native American population already present. Matthew Thornton subsequently became the last signer of the Declaration of Independence. Following the discussions that would include the Matthew Thornton name, Thornton Oaks was selected to be the name of the new retirement community.

The management of MCHS hired a consultant to research and propose a financial structure for this new community and find an ownership model, which gave the hospital meaningful control of the quality of the community without an equity investment. The result was the Homeowners Cooperative ownership model with management of the cooperative residing with MCHS. Demographic studies were conducted to further clarify the demand for the retirement community. All studies pointed to the unmet needs, and a plan was developed to move ahead with board approval.

At this time a crucial yet little known land agreement came about as a result of a discussion which occurred 20 years earlier between long-time Brunswick journalist and hospital leader Harry G. Shulman and Henry M. Baribeau, a real estate agency owner. On a handshake Baribeau agreed that he would give Regional Memorial Hospital first refusal if he divested himself of any future holdings on Baribeau Drive. Baribeau called Paris to explain the discussion and asked if the hospital was interested in the sale. For the sum of $75,000, the hospital purchased forty acres of land adjacent to the hospital property. Twenty nine acres were deeded by the hospital on a long-term lease to the Thornton Oaks Development Corporation. The financial model adopted was successful, allowing residents to have equity ownership of their home or apartment and at the same time know that the

MCHS will always have a stewardship role in the community.

Joining Mid Coast Hospital in moving the project forward was Coventry Resources, a Maryland based company specializing in retirement communities and Barry, Bette, and Leduc, a construction company from Albany, New York that brought financial guarantees and construction expertise to the project. MCHS remained the managing partner of this project.

The late 1980s were a challenging time for the banking systems in this country and local banks were not immune to tight regulations. Mid Coast Hospital applied for a construction loan through Northeast Bank in Brunswick for $900,000. As equity, Mid Coast Hospital provided a guarantee in pre-sales of one half of the first phase of the project, which was 26 private cottages. Half of these cottages were pre-sold and secured by a 10% deposit. The hospital had loaned the Thornton Oaks Development Corporation close to $1 million for the development of infrastructure, architectural drawings, engineering drawings and legal documents. At the 11th hour the bank demanded an additional $400,000 in equity. Five individuals from the community—Herbert Paris, Richard A. Morrell, Frank Crooker, Frank Goodwin and Campbell B. Niven, each signed a promissory note of $80,000. They received no financial reward of any kind for this act of generosity and this satisfied the demand of the bank for the $400,000. The promissory notes were never called and the notes were discharged two years later. Van McCullough was appointed executive director of Thornton Oaks in 1993 and over the next 17 years provided stability and leadership to this growing community. Forty six private homes were fully subscribed by 1994, followed by the groundbreaking for the large 100 unit apartment house, Matthew Terrace. When the project was fully developed, the Homeowners Corporation became the project owner, and MCHS continued to serve in the contract management capacity.

LONG TERM CARE BEDS: MERE POINT NURSING HOME
In response to the anticipated needs for long term care beds, Mid Coast Hospital acquired Mere Point Nursing Home, an older 26-bed facility located on Mere Point Road in Brunswick in 1989. The long term plan for the facility was to eventually relocate the beds to Regional Memorial Hospital once its acute care services were moved to a new hospital.

Mid Coast Hospital found itself moving successfully beyond acute care services with the Thornton Oaks project and the Mere Point Nursing Home acquisition. However, these two elements left Mid Coast Hospital far from its vision of a full continuum of resources serving the communities' overall health needs.

DEACONESS HOSPITAL,
BOSTON, MA

Bath Maternal Child Clinic 1930s. Ruth Weeks Henry RN, *Philomena Eramos, and her mother Dominica Eramos*

HOME HEALTH SERVICES: COMMUNITY HEALTH AND NURSING
SERVICES (CHANS)

When Red Cross nurse Ruth Weeks Henry came to Bath in 1931, it is doubtful anyone knew the adventures and difficulties that preceded her arrival. A graduate of Deaconess School of Nursing in 1914, she served in France during WWI with Base Hospital No. 5 (Harvard Unit). A quiet and professional person by all accounts, Mrs. Henry moved into the Cosmolitan Club, a home for single women and began her community nursing career which spanned over twenty five years. Her work included caring for the sick and post partum at home, holding weekly well-child clinics, and assisting the state physician with tuberculosis and sexually transmitted disease screening and follow up. In the 1940s she also drove youngsters with polio to Lewiston for physician care and helped school nurses with immunization clinics. (33)

When in 1947, the Red Cross returned the agency to the community, the Public Health Nursing Service was formed in Bath. With the help of community minded citizens Mary Guild, John Cary, Anna Sewall, Julie Musk and others, the agency was born. This organization was the precursor of Community Health and Nursing Services (CHANS), which considered Ruth Weeks Henry its founder. Following several moves of its facilities and financial troubles, the opportunity arose in 1987 for an affiliation and ultimately a merger with Mid Coast Health Services. Regional Memorial Hospital developed a free-standing office building on its campus to house CHANS under a long-term lease agreement. The hospital's willingness to serve as a source of credit to develop the facility for CHANS represented an act of good faith, and not a measured step toward an integrated community health care delivery system that Regional Memorial Hospital was envisioning. However, following CHANS' occupancy of its facility, the executive director became terminally ill. This time CHANS was

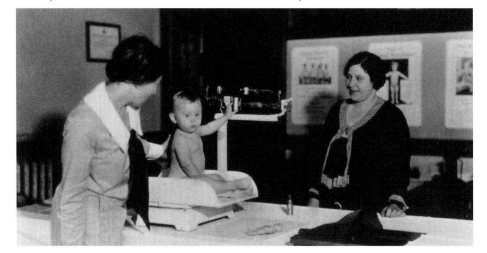

Doris Watson RN, director
of Bath/Brunswick
Regional Health Agency

CHANS 1976
4 Park Street, Bath

CHANS 1982
32 Hennessey Avenue, Brunswick

Robert Liversidge,
first CHANS director 1973–82

CHANS 1987, 50 Baribeau Drive, Brunswick

Laura Cathcart RN,
director 1982–87

Jean St. Amand RN, director 1992–97

Juliana L'Heureux RN
director 1997–2005

*Physical Therapist
Jeanette Boudin with
patient 1976*

facing severe operational and working capital problems. When
the CHANS board began to discuss its options in terms of new
leadership, Hodgdon, serving as a member of the CHANS board,
said the holding company would be willing to assume responsibility for management of the agency. Paris followed up with
a call to the chairman of the CHANS board. The message was
simple: Paris suggested that before CHANS was forced to go out
of business they should sit down and talk.

In 1992, the Mid Coast Hospital board expressed its willingness to explore a merger with CHANS. The agreement reached was
that Mid Coast Hospital would enter into a six month management contract, during which time it would work to turn the operational and financial performance of CHANS around. At the end
of the six months, both organizations would assess linking CHANS
as a not-for-profit subsidiary of Mid Coast Health Services.

In 1993, the CHANS board was discharged with appreciation and
thanks and a new nine-member board was appointed—four from the
former CHANS board and five from MCHS. Tough decisions still had to
be made. Worthwhile services that were losing substantial amounts of
money needed to be curtailed or eliminated. Staffing changes needed
to be made. The end result was a stable home health company that was
well positioned to contribute services, planning, and operations within
an integrated system that encompassed acute, long-term and supportive
living, as well as being a key ingredient in the continuum of care that
Mid Coast Hospital had embraced.

In 2005 CHANS moved to 60 Baribeau Drive, the remodeled
Regional Memorial Hospital, and came under the leadership of
Darlene Chalmers RN, executive director of the Senior Health Center.

HOSPICE

In 2009 the Hospice volunteer organization approached Mid Coast Hospital
to begin discussions about how the two organizations could come together.
Hospice volunteers and CHANS had a long relationship extending over a
period of years. The Hospice volunteers' mission was to "provide caring,
supportive, non-medical services to individuals, families and community
organizations coping with dying and grief, as well as education and dialogue
within the community about end of life services." CHANS, which had
earlier become the Medicare certified Hospice program under the leadership
of Laura Cathcart RN embraced this mission and committed itself to
the personal, caring and compassionate clinical services to complement
the supportive services provided by the Hospice volunteers. The two

organizations joined forces and Hospice was integrated into CHANS in 2010. The program continues to thrive and grow.

VISION OF A SINGLE HOSPITAL

Following the merger of Bath and Regional hospitals to form Mid Coast Hospital, the board planning committee explored a vision set forth by administration. This eventually called for the building of a new single facility to replace the two existing hospitals, to reduce its inpatient capacity and return the associated savings to the community in the form of reduced pricing. Maine had a Certificate of Need (C.O.N.) regulation requiring review and approval of capital projects exceeding $1 million by the Department of Human Services. The preparation of such an application was mandatory.

Nearly a year and a half before the application was delivered for review a series of meetings were held with the C.O.N. regulators. Clearly with a project of this scale, open lines of communications would be essential to ensure a complete application and an informed and accurate review.

To kick off the planning, Payette Associates, a Boston architectural firm, was engaged to develop the conceptual design of the proposed new hospital.

The real strength of the application was not the document itself, but rather the extensive, broad-based planning process upon which it rested. The clear vision of the new Mid Coast Hospital was of a community hospital, not a tertiary center. Community, physician, and employee input reflected a carefully measured response to a well defined community need projecting several decades into the future.

In preparing the Certificate of Need to make the case for a single hospital, over 12 approaches were conceptualized, including collaboration with Parkview Memorial Hospital.

Eventually four different approaches were studied: 1) maintain the status quo of a two campus delivery system; 2) consolidate all acute care services at the Bath Memorial Hospital; 3) consolidate all acute care services at the Regional Memorial Hospital; and 4) develop a new hospital facility on a new centrally located campus.

Once the study options were identified, the next question was what criteria should be used to determine a solution. Cost, quality and access were acknowledged as legitimate criteria, and given the pre-eminence of local, state, and national health cost issues. Cost had to be the focal point.

This approach offered the most objective quantifiable standard for comparison among the four options. At first blush, comparing each option on the basis of its relative cost to the community seemed straight forward, but this soon became a very complex task.

Discarded was the concept of developing traditional profit/loss projections for each, because of the difficulty of accurately predicting revenues into the near future, let alone ten years in the future. Changes in Medicare, Medicaid, Blue Cross, and managed care could easily nullify the conclusions of the most sensitive revenue predictions.

Once a unit cost approach was agreed upon, a method for developing both volume and expense projections was created. Each option was modeled using demand scenarios that detailed service volume assumptions as driven by marketshare, length of stay, medical staff development and new technology. To accurately account for the impact of outpatients, an industry standard, "cost per adjusted admission" was utilized.

As service volume assumptions were being generated, capital and operating cost assumptions needed to be developed to generate unit costs that would be incurred for refurbishing and expanding the existing facilities, if either was used as the initial structure for the consolidation of the two facilities. These scenarios tried to anticipate the need to accommodate outpatient services growth within each facility. In many respects, estimating costs for new construction was easier than renovation costs for existing campuses.

Operating expense assumptions were generated by building a model that treated fixed and variable costs separately. Fixed costs of facilities stayed constant despite any change in volume assumptions. In contrast, as volume and acuity assumptions were changed, variable costs reacted up and down within this model. When each option was completed and run, provocative findings began to emerge. In essence the numbers were showing that the least expensive solutions to a unit of service cost basis was the new hospital. This was the final recommendation that resulted from this methodology.

The Certificate of Need application proposed that Mid Coast Hospital build a new facility to replace its two existing hospitals, to reduce its capacity from 145 beds to 104 beds, and to return the associated savings to the community in the form of reduced prices. This 1993 c.o.n. application was contested and challenged by Parkview Hospital in a public hearing on the basis that the new hospital should be built without obstetrical beds. Mid Coast Hospital had 14 obstetrical beds at the Bath facility. Parkview's contention was that it had sufficient obstetrical beds to meet the needs of the region. Jane Sheehan, the sitting commissioner of the Department of Human Services (DHS), issued a Certificate of Need authorization for the $38 million project to proceed with the condition that no obstetrical beds be involved. This action destroyed the financial feasibility of the entire project and ignored the statutory and regulatory requirements which the DHS must meet for C.O.N. review, and ran directly counter to the Department's published standards and criteria related to obstetrical services. The decision of the commissioner left considerable doubt whether or not the project would proceed.

Indeed, Mid Coast indicated that it would not build the new hospital without an obstetrical service. Following meetings with the commissioner to clarify the reasons for her decision, we were advised that there would be no further comment coming forth from the then sitting commissioner, and if we wished to explore further appeals that we could do so with the new administration that would take office in six months.

The resolution to this dilemma was for the hospital leadership to wait until the new state administration was in place, and after a reasonable period of time, the hospital appealed to the new commissioner for an interpretation of what the previous commissioner had ordered in approving the C.O.N. without obstetrical beds. The basic question was whether or not Mid Coast Hospital could deliver babies in the future. The decision of the new commissioner, Kevin Concannon, determined that Mid Coast could proceed with the provision of obstetrical care to patients, however, any beds for the obstetrical service could not be "dedicated beds," but the beds could also be used for other patients. The decision was made at that point to proceed with the planning based on the concept of the development of a women's health service that would not only include obstetrical care but also care of women in general who required hospitalization and who could be intermingled in an environment that was also a maternity unit.

When the commissioner's interpretation was received by Parkview the decision clearly was not the answer they wanted or expected. Parkview's response was to launch a court challenge as an affected third party that was not given an opportunity to provide input into this decision. Both the commissioner and Mid Coast Hospital were named as defendants in the suit.

During a long and perplexing period of time that lasted from 1993 through 1997, the court battle took MCHS through the Superior Court where a quick and judgmental decision was made without benefit of deliberations by the then sitting Superior Court Justice Leigh Saufley. She upheld the decision of the first commissioner to not allow obstetrical beds in the new hospital—this was a significant setback for Mid Coast Hospital.

After this decision in Superior Court an appeal was made to the State of Maine Supreme Court. Six months passed with no decision in sight. To the surprise of Mid Coast Hospital, the principal challenger, Parkview, withdrew any challenge against obstetrical beds in the new hospital, and indicated that it had no further opposition to the new hospital. A joint statement was released between Mid Coast Hospital and Parkview Hospital indicating there was no further challenge to the project and it would proceed. This action required a return to the Superior Court with a request that Justice Leigh Saufley's decision be vacated followed by a request to the Supreme Court to withdraw the appeal of the Superior Court decision and to erase the matter from the record. It was Parkview's request that the matter be erased from the public record and Parkview not be seen as the obstructionist to the development of the new Mid Coast Hospital.

In the same time frame, it became increasingly obvious that without the new hospital on the horizon, services would continue to be provided in duplicate between the Bath and Brunswick campuses. We were running duplicate services on all inpatient care activities with the exception of obstetrics in Bath and psychiatry in Brunswick. Without resolution to the new hospital proceeding, we would begin to turn the financial gains of the merger into significant losses.

Internal discussions involving the medical staff and board of directors determined that in order to preserve our financial stability and to move ahead with the new hospital we had to capture whatever savings we could as a result of the merger. The conclusion reached was that all inpatient services be consolidated on the Brunswick campus. The obvious

reasons were that our principal competition was in Brunswick and if we left the Brunswick scene it would be detrimental to the future growth of Mid Coast Hospital. The second was that the facilities in Brunswick were better, newer, and provided the additional room for expansion, whereas the Bath facility had limited opportunities for expansion. The decision included placing all inpatient medical, surgical, pediatrics, ICU, psychiatry and maternity inpatient services in Brunswick supported by a 24 hour emergency room, rehabilitation services, lab, X-ray and ambulatory surgical services. The Bath facility would have a large primary care physician office practice occupying the building as well as a walk-in urgent care center and a full array of outpatient and rehabilitation services. It was decided that the move would be announced in late summer of 1996, with the expected implementation occurring in October of 1997. This would allow a year of planning to make the transition as smooth as possible.

Hospital representatives then went to the City of Bath in an open meeting held at Bath City Hall to present plans to the City Council and assembled citizens. The City Council was clearly upset that it was not involved earlier in the process, even though it was to take place a year later. Councilors did not believe the numbers of the potential financial loss without consolidation. A loss would prohibit the ability to finance a new hospital since it would absorb much of our assets planned to be put into the new hospital. A lack of trust surfaced as to the hospital's motives and many felt that the primary reason for the consolidation was to eliminate the Bath facility and move everything to Brunswick. The City Council then asked that the decision be put on hold. The hospital was not prepared to put this decision on hold beyond a specified period of time. Hospital officials agreed to not make the final decision until there was an opportunity to review again the full scale of the project with the City of Bath.

Throughout the summer, hospital personnel met with the City of Bath and surrounding communities with extensive studies and negotiations taking place. The City of Bath decided to call in a consultant to review the financial statements of Mid Coast Hospital and in his final review, the consultant found that the hospital was in a strong financial condition and that indeed the hospital's records were in order. The City hired a mediator to seek resolution, aimed toward the effort to keep the Bath hospital open.

At the conclusion of three months of intensive discussions, the hard decision was made by Mid Coast Hospital that it could wait no longer and at that point undertook the initial work required to begin the preparation of the Brunswick site for the consolidation of all inpatient services. The most important need was to build a new obstetrical unit. Inquiry

STATE OF MAINE

SUPREME JUDICIAL COURT   Docket No. CUM-96-303
Sitting as the Law Court

PARKVIEW HOSPITAL   )
)
)
            v.   )   ORDER ON JOINT MOTION TO
)   DISMISS THE APPEAL AND TO
)   VACATE THE DECISION OF THE
COMMISSIONER OF HUMAN   )   SUPERIOR COURT AND TO
SERVICES   )   DISMISS THE ACTION
)
and   )
)
MID COAST HOSPITAL   )

On the Joint Motion of Parkview Hospital and Midcoast Hospital, and without objection by the Commissioner of Human Services, the Motion is granted in part:

The appeal of the Commissioner and Midcoast is dismissed, without prejudice, and the case remanded to the Superior Court for further proceedings.

Dated: March 24, 1997

RECEIVED

MAR 24 1997

SUPREME JUDICIAL COURT

For the Court,

Daniel E. Wathen

Daniel E. Wathen, Chief Justice

was made to the DHS on the requirement of a C.O.N. to move a hospital service from one community to another, if it was part of the same hospital. DHS indicated that a C.O.N. was not necessary and the hospital proceeded with the project with the expense coming under the threshold in which a C.O.N. is required. Without a C.O.N. the project could not be challenged by Parkview Adventist Medical Center. This was strategically important since the unit was not a long term investment, but an interim step to the new hospital.

Much anger and hostility was displayed by the Bath community over

```
STATE OF MAINE                              SUPERIOR COURT
CUMBERLAND, SS                              CIVIL ACTION
                                            DOCKET NO. CV 95-374

PARKVIEW HOSPITAL,                    )
                                      )
              Petitioner              )
                                      )
      v.                              )
                                      )    ORDER
COMMISSIONER OF HUMAN SERVICES        )
      and                             )
MID COAST HOSPITAL                    )
                                      )
              Respondents             )
```

On the joint motion of Parkview Hospital and Mid Coast Hospital, and the Commissioner of Human Services having indicted his consent to that motion, it is hereby

ORDERED

That the Court's Order of April 2, 1996 is hereby vacated and that this action is hereby dismissed with prejudice and without costs to any party.

Dated: _3/27/97_

Leigh Saufley, Justice
Superior Court

smith\jmrp\mch\24900003 order on mo to vacate

the loss of its inpatient hospital services. Hospital leadership continued to take the high road by explaining repeatedly why this move was necessary if, indeed, it was ultimately going to get to the new hospital. Some proposed that the idea of a new hospital was a ploy and there was no intention of ever building a new facility.

Shortly after the consolidation of the services in Brunswick, the board of directors again engaged Ernst and Young to conduct a feasibility study to review and determine if there were any significant changes in the initial financial forecast which would challenge moving ahead. Their engagement prepared the financial forecast for the five years ending in 2002, which would include one year of the new hospital operation. In reviewing the assumptions of service area definition, market share growth, volume, payor mix, full time equivalent employees, inflation, fundraising, third party bond sizing of working capital, Ernst and Young results showed that the hospital's financial condition had not deteriorated. The changes in the market share from increased penetration appeared reasonable. Salary and non-salary inflations appeared aggressive but management would be able to control these inflations. The hospital had appropriate debt service coverage for the bond issue. The recommendation was to move ahead with the development of the new

hospital as soon as possible. Indeed, if the hospital did not move ahead it would have serious financial as well as service implications. (34) The board made the decision to proceed in all haste with the planning and development of a new facility on the land that had been purchased in East Brunswick in 1988, the eventual new home of Mid Coast Hospital.

THE PLAN

After the successful fund drive for land years before, led by John Morse, Jr., a hospital fundraising financial feasibility study was initiated with 75 residents of the communities interviewed on whether the hospital should proceed with the new facility, and if so, would there be adequate fundraising support. Information gained indicated strong support and a generous financial response could be expected from the communities. Armed with these results, a fundraising committee formed under the able chairmanship of Campbell B. Niven, a fundraising counsel was engaged and a host of volunteer solicitors began with a goal of $4.5 million. Ultimately the fundraising drive was so successful that the goal was raised to $6 million and $6.5 million was finally raised. Concurrent with this campaign were decisions to hire a hospital planner and a project architect, the two efforts to proceed in tandem and done by two separate

organizations. The previous design of the
new hospital by Payette Associates was
abandoned. The firm of Shepley, Bulfinch,
Richardson and Abbott of Boston was
hired to be the architect and Lammers +
Associates, Inc. of Virginia, the planner.

The planner had a year to determine the
space, adjacencies, and physical size of the
facility, with the architect, a member of
the team, however not the leader. The plan
then went to the architects to develop the
design. An important aspect of the team
was the addition of a construction manager to constantly assess the cost to assure
that the building was within the allocated
c.o.n. budget. Construction manager was
H.P. Cummings, a Maine based construction company.

The basic factor impacting the design
was the $38.5 million authorized in the
c.o.n. approval in 1993. There was no al-
lowance for inflation during the four year
delay due to the challenge by Parkview
and the appeal process. Ultimately, the

I**N**
CELEBRATION

**Marking a milestone
in health care
for our communities**

Groundbreaking for the new Mid Coast Hospital
September 16, 1999 • Brunswick, Maine

hospital design was reduced to 72 beds with a full outpatient capacity. Also very important was the decision that a Medical Office Building could be constructed at a much lower cost because no expensive technical or code factors had to be met. Developer David Schlosser of Healthsettings, Inc., Rochester, N.Y., agreed to build a connected office building, in a design similar to that of the hospital. This would allow a seamless interaction between the hospital and the medical office building. The hospital would lease space to provide administration, conference rooms, cafeteria and other support services, in addition to physician's offices, separately leased by the individual practices.

In the four years between the initial submission of the c.o.n. and the final authority to proceed, a major redesign of the hospital was necessary. Significant changes had taken place in the delivery and utilization of hospital services. Outpatient surgery, for example, had rapidly replaced a large number of inpatient procedures and there was rapid advancement of new technical equipment. Insurance companies developed reforms to cover many outpatient procedures and the length of stay was shortened. These external changes in practice and payment required rethinking in the design of how hospital services would be delivered in the future.

The silver lining to the dark cloud of delay was that significant external changes had taken place and the original design of the hospital would not have accommodated those changes. We would have built a hospital reflecting the past rather than a hospital for the future.

9

The HEALING
ENVIRONMENT

Tʜᴇ ᴛᴡᴏ ᴄᴏᴍᴍᴜɴɪᴛʏ ʜᴏsᴘɪᴛᴀʟs that had served the greater Bath/
Brunswick area were both examples of inefficient, outdated design
and dreary décor. But this was not uncommon during the era that these
were built. While we should have been aware in the 1950s that the lay-
out and surroundings of the hospital would translate into better care for
patients, it was not part of the culture. Hospitals were well known for
their institutional feel, with dingy beige walls, fluorescent lighting, and
cramped patient rooms.

In 1859 Florence Nightingale noted in her writing the healing effect of
color, light, noise control, warmth and cleanliness.

> *"To any but an old nurse or an old patient the degree would be
> quite inconceivable to which the nerves of the sick suffer from
> seeing the same walls, the same ceiling, and the same surround-
> ings during a long confinement in one or two rooms. The nervous
> frame suffers too. The effect on sickness of beautiful objects, a
> variety of objects, and especially a brilliancy of color is hardly
> at all appreciated. I have seen in fevers, the most acute suffering
> produced from the patient not being able to see out of a window;
> the knots in the wood being the only view. I shall never forget
> the rapture of fever patients over a bunch of brilliantly colored*

flowers. People say the effect is only on the mind. The effect is on the body too. Little as we know about the way in which we are affected by form, color, and light, we do know this, that they have an actual physical effect. Variety, form and brilliancy in color in the objects presented to patients are actual means of recovery." (35)

The leadership and staff at Mid Coast Hospital had the opportunity of designing the first new hospital in Maine in 25 years. Much thought had been given to the selection of a site, located on an estuary of the New Meadows River, which flows out into the Atlantic Ocean. With the 155 acres of pristine woodland, the architects had the advantage of sighting the hospital to make the best use of the natural environment. The vision of creating a healing environment was to balance the remarkable 21st century and scientific advances in health care with the more traditional and human aspects of healing. We sought to bring comfort, beauty and peace of mind to people of all ages with diverse life experiences, while celebrating mid coast Maine's cultural heritage. In doing so, we hoped to create an environment that heals each patient as a whole person—body, mind and spirit.

The creation of Mid Coast Hospital with a focus on the healing environment was very much a collaborative approach involving a symbiotic relationship between the architects, the hospital and the healing environment committee. The committee, chaired by Dr. William Clark, an internist, included physicians, artists, employees and community members who worked closely together, not only to address what kind of art could best be introduced into the hospital, but how the art could be most enhanced by color, lighting and other elements that were within the architects' responsibility. We began the project by first educating ourselves on the effects of art in a hospital environment. We invited the entire hospital staff—including physicians and trustees—to participate. Soft colors and textures, natural and subdued light, carpets and personal pagers replaced institutional lighting, formica and noisy overhead paging. Patients have mostly private rooms with ample space for the clinical team, family and friends—a general atmosphere less threatening and more inviting. Also important was the understanding that a healing environment accounts for the needs of the staff as well as patients and families. The healing environment committee took on the responsibility to develop the criteria for art acquisition.

Patients have always complained that they experienced a sense of helplessness and loss of self in the hospital. In the early 1980s Harriet Paris had selected and hung artwork at Regional which initiated the

Tiles made by area fourth graders decorate public space throughout Mid Coast Hospital

Harriet Paris selected and coordinated placement of the visual arts throughout Mid Coast Health Services.

Four Quartets, *2001*
Mark Wethli, Kyle
Durrie and Cassie Jones

New Born, *1961*
William Zorach

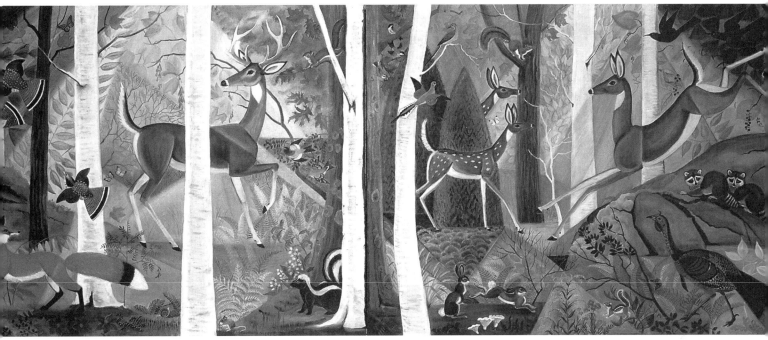

October Woods, *2001 Dahlov Ipcar*

concept of the healing environment philosophy. The healing environment project proposed to embrace the arts in the new hospital in a significant way and to provide spaces, symbols, and surroundings that would encourage the joining of caring for patients and staff. The architectural team and the building committee embraced, encouraged and supported this concept. Introduced into the hospital were significant works of art including sculpture, paintings, glass works, murals and architecturally designed space and colors to enhance the artwork.

Painted tiles were produced by 4th grade students from schools in the hospital's service area. Children created over 800 tiles which were mounted and hung in clusters in the patient units and public areas. Painting these tiles gave a sense of ownership to a future generation, many of whom will make their homes in mid coast Maine. The students' tile projects also gave school staff an opportunity to discuss illness and caring with the students in preparation for their artistic expression.

An individual project was undertaken by Harriet Paris, a volunteer on the healing environment committee, to select, frame and hang museum reproductions in all patient rooms, patient corridors, and hospital support depart-

Charles Richelieu

Robert McCue

Lois Skillings

Philip Ortolani

ments. Visual art was placed throughout the entire hospital and adjoining medical office building. The committee spent a great deal of time discussing what should be the initial impression when people walked into the hospital front entrance. Traditionally, the lobby and main corridors in the hospital world have lists of donors and plaques reflecting people's generosity. We were probably heading in that same direction in Brunswick, until the healing environment committee made a recommendation that an inviting piece of art should grace the front entrance lobby in a very significant way. Similarly, this concept held true for all of the main public corridors.

Following extensive design, planning and development, construction was finally undertaken and scheduled to be completed in December, 2001, a 36-month construction period. A building committee chaired by Charles Richelieu, a member of the board of directors, brought commitment and discipline to the project and a careful monitoring system for budget control. The building was completed on schedule and under budget. The chief engineering officer and director of physical plant, Michael Pinkham, served as clerk of the works and brought continuity and institutional memory to the project. Philip Ortolani, Vice President for Operations, brought structure to the space planning phase and Robert McCue, Chief Financial Officer, kept tight control over the budget.

THE TRANSITION

Fourteen months prior to the anticipated completion of the new hospital, transition planning began. A consultant was hired to help us with the overall transition planning effort, and a transition committee was formed and chaired by Lois Skillings, Vice President for Nursing and Patient Care Services. Darlene Chalmers RN was charged with the overall coordination of the move to the new facility. The committee was responsible for the overall planning, budgeting, communications, operational readiness, staff orientation and then to actually implement the transition and move patients from the old to the new. Subcommittees planned, developed and implemented all the details of the move.

The single overriding focus was patient safety with potential risks including: a new environment of care, completely new processes and systems, move of equipment, dual operation of departments during the actual period of the move, possible lack of communications, and then finally the actual move of patients. Established to accomplish this included seven teams appointed by the transition steering committee: an operational development committee charged with developing the concepts of operation during the move; staffing needs and human resources; develop-

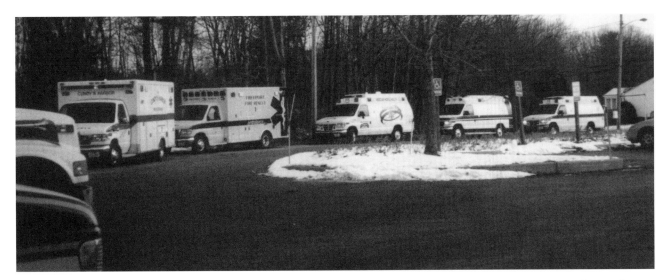

Moving day, December 11, 2001

ment of hospital-wide programs, policies and procedures; planning for a run-through of "A Day in the Life" in the new hospital; and finally the reintegration of our staff and patients in the new facility. The transition goals were to provide the community with safe, high quality patient care without interruption before, during, and after the patient move; to create staff ownership of the process and to provide organization and accountability of all resources, to create integration of activities, and lastly to provide documentation and communications for the plan.

Public events included the groundbreaking, periodic tours during construction, the dedication, community open house, Mid Coast employee and family open houses, a gala ball, a road race and a continuing series of guided tours that went on several days a week. Weekend tours were conducted by volunteer guides. The medical staff was fully engaged in the orientation to the new facility. On November 30th, 2001, a huge celebratory event, "The Tower Ball," took place under the auspices of the Auxiliary. An enormous tent was erected in the parking lot connected by canvas walkways to the hospital. Since it was November, large heaters blew in hot air and close to 1,000 members of the community, from all walks of life, gathered in formal clothing to feast and dance the night away to two bands. A formal dedication was held two days later on Sunday, December 2nd and the first patients were transferred on December 11th, 2001. Careful planning and communications provided alternative plans, if there was snow and ice. While this would not stop the move itself, adequate provision was made in each case for the safe transfer of patients. Local ambulances, municipal volunteers and private services, all volunteered their time and vehicles to help with the move. The education and orientation plans involved everyone that was in any way involved with the hospital. As a result the move was smooth and without incident. At 6:00 a.m. on

Michael Pinkham

Darlene Chalmers RN

December 11th the first patient left the old hospital by ambulance and the new Mid Coast Hospital was officially opened. The entire move took place over a six-hour period. The old hospital was closed and the new hospital was opened in a simultaneous action.

As part of the overall plan it was important to have an effective reuse of the Regional and Bath Hospitals. To this end, Regional Hospital was transformed into a senior health center and the Bath Hospital was sold to the City of Bath for one dollar.

To provide for the senior health center, $10 million dollars was invested in the remodeling. The new construction resulted in a 21-bed rehabilitation unit, to continue to be known as the Bodwell Unit. A long term care facility of 21 beds to be known as the Mere Point Nursing Center, a 14 bed memory impairment facility, to be known as The Garden, and 39 assisted living apartments known as Thornton Hall. This facility was connected by a covered walk-way to Thornton Oaks Retirement Community, thus enabling the continuum to be reinforced between independent living, assisted living, memory impairment, rehabilitation, long-term care and hospice care. The Senior Health Center was enhanced by gifts from Richard and Shana Donnell for an outdoor deck and comfortable hospice care rooms and a gift from Robert Brownell of a garden in memory of his wife Mary Scootie Brownell, a long-time voluneer at the hospital.

The Bath hospital became the focus of a series of discussions on how it might best be reused. The final conclusion was reached when the board of Mid Coast sold the hospital to the City of Bath. State Senator Arthur Mayo, representing Bath in the Maine State Legislature, took a leadership role, and procured a commitment from the legislature of $1 million dollars to remodel the Bath Hospital and prepare it for use as a campus for Southern Maine Community College. The hospital agreed to be an anchor tenant with a long-term lease for the Bath primary care physicians of the Mid Coast Medical Group.

10

VOLUNTEERISM

VOLUNTEERISM HAS PLAYED an important role in the development of the hospital system in America, since the transition from the Alms houses in the 17th century to the beginnings of the voluntary hospital system in the 18th century. This tradition was embraced in the growth and development of the Bath Memorial Hospital, Regional Memorial Hospital and the Mid Coast Hospital and created a threshold between the hospital and the community. The community volunteerism, which bene-fited the hospitals over the years, extended beyond the founders, boards of directors and corporators. In the early days of the hospitals, local families and benevolent organizations started a tradition of endowing rooms to assure that they were properly and decoratively equipped.

The Bath Hospital minutes record this activity and document the benevolence of: the San Souci Club, the Small Point Colony, the Mon-day Club, the Lions, the Plummer family, the Stetson family, Dearborn family, and the Nightingale Club among others. Donation week was held annually in Bath in November, to collect fruit, vegetables, jellies, sweets and financial contributions from the community. The annual report of the Bath hospital in 1921 states that many church organizations and societies had made sheets.

Volunteerism oriented to patient care and patient well-being is first documented in February 1924, when the Bath board president William D.

Sewall suggested to the ladies of Bath, the advisability of occasionally calling at the hospital—"such a policy would be appreciated by the inmates...." Later that year the "women of the board" held a street fair chaired by trustee Mrs. John A. Morse. In October, the president asked the ladies to call "especially on the superintendent and the staff giving them encouragement." The first auxiliary activities began late that year in the form of a junior sewing club, which enlisted girls to assist with the sewing of hospital linens. At the time, bandages, sheets, blankets and towels were constructed in house.

During the first quarter of the 20th century, a movement to encourage young women to form charitable, not-for-profit organizations to benefit their communities took hold in Bath, and the Bath Junior League was born. The first mention of "junior members" is made in the trustees' minutes of September 1925, in which it was noted that a card party had earned $250 for the hospital. The hospital Junior League immediately formed and held a successful New Year's Eve Ball. In September of 1927 *The Bath Times* reported that the League had raised $800 through "social functions" such as card parties, dances and sewing. With 20 members, soon

High Fever Follies Committee of the Bath Junior Hospital League, 1962.

Seated: Mrs. Melvin Henderson (Di Francis), Mrs. Oscar March (Suzi), and Mrs. Lawrence Katz (Sylvia). Standing: Mrs. Warren Howley (Esther), Mrs. Courtney Stover (Ida), Mrs. John Allen (Skippy), Mrs. Edson Whitechurst (Judy), Mrs. Dean Shaw (Marion), Mrs. Rosalys Kondos, Mrs. William Haggett (Sally).

MAINE MARITIME MUSEUM

Hi Fever Follies

PRESENTED BY
THE BATH MEMORIAL
HOSPITAL AUXILIARY

FALL
1960

The Bath Memorial Auxiliary operated a Front Street Thrift Shop called The Clearing House in the 1950 and 60 decades.

after World War I, the league's objectives were to raise money through fundraising projects and to promote the interests of the hospital in every possible way. While it began for social reasons, the Junior League always had a charitable mission and began to devote all of their efforts to aid the Bath Hospital, contributing many needed pieces of medical equipment including the first Kelvinator refrigerator. In the late 1940s the League began its most notable and prolific fund raising strategy: the Bath Antique Show, chaired for thirty six years by Janet Bridgham Bussey, who was also the first female Bath Memorial Hospital board chairman. According to Antique Show Co-chair Marion Redlon, the event often earned $12,000 in the 1960s and '70s. The League disbanded in 1990 when the two hospitals merged.

In 1932, eight women organized the Nightingale Club sewing baby clothes, blankets, dresser scarves and the like for the hospital. The club was active for forty four years, disbanding in 1976. In 1944, the major project was to organize the hospital auxiliary, which, by the 1960s, grew to a size of nearly 400 members. Activities of the Bath Auxiliary in the late 1940s included an annual "Old Thyme Fair," organizing "on duty ward service" volunteers, and making bandages. In the 1950s the Auxiliary opened a small "Cozy Corner" gift shop in the hospital lobby and a downtown thrift shop called the "Clearing House." In the 1960s the group opened a lucrative Coffee Shop and began a string of annual talent shows called "The Hi Fever Follies." The Bath Auxiliary continued its major volunteer focus through the 1990s.

The Regional Hospital Auxiliary had its beginning in the mid 1950s, when a group of volunteers at the old Brunswick Community Hospital organized to form a volunteer core. That group subsequently became the Auxiliary of the Regional Memorial Hospital when it opened in 1960 with Mrs. Louise Abelon serving as the first president. Again, the focus of the Regional Auxiliary was to support the hospital through a variety of different fund raising efforts. In 1960 the thrift shop opened downtown under the name of 'Second Hand Rose' with the leadership of Dorothy Stetson, Lucy Shulman and Dolly Ladd. Volunteers basically were members who lived in downtown Brunswick and could easily walk to the thrift shop. In 1968, a major effort entitled "Hospitaliday" was planned and conducted on the Bowdoin campus, and in one day the Auxiliary raised $50,000 to equip the new Intensive Care Unit.

The next major undertaking of the Brunswick Auxiliary was the snack bar, under the leadership of Eleanor (Smokey) Morrell, located in a corner of the lobby entrance of the 1960s. When the 1982 wing was built, a new coffee shop opened to accommodate the needs of visitors and staff, and a new gift shop opened under the leadership of Elizabeth (Betsy) Niven and Helen Hunter.

With the merger in the early 1990s, the two auxiliaries began working together, although they remained separate entities until the new hospital was ready to open. They officially merged in October 2001, to become a single Mid Coast Hospital Auxiliary.

As the completion of the new hospital approached the Auxiliary organized the "Tower Ball," a major grand social event that celebrated the opening with close to 1,000 people in black tie and evening wear. A very significant amount of money was raised for the pledge of $400,000 that the Bath and Brunswick Auxiliaries had made toward the capital campaign. The auxiliary continued to grow significantly to encompass 500 men and women who provide services in every area—both patient care areas and support areas of the hospital. Volunteer service is a vital part of the patient care programs at the hospital and it includes junior volunteers (high school students formally known as candy stripers) during the summer recess and Bowdoin College students during the academic year. This service has grown under the capable direction of Millie Stewart, director of volunteers.

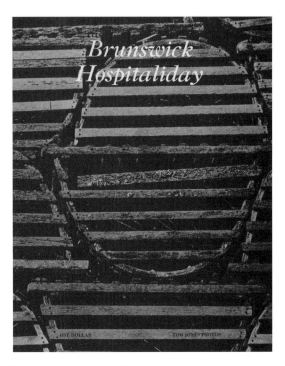

Regional Memorial Auxiliary sold this booklet of photographs by Tom Jones to raise funds in 1968.

Millie Stewart

11

PROMOTING *a*
HEALTHY COMMUNITY

B ATH, REGIONAL AND MID COAST Hospitals have had a long tradition of promoting the health and wellness of the community as part
of their missions, with programs taking a variety of forms.

RUNNING START

Peter Evans MD, an internist on the Regional medical staff, is credited
with providing the impetus and leadership to develop a program to help
cardiac patients make a faster recovery. For many years the post myocar-
dial infarction patient endured a six-week hospitalization and was often
considered disabled; this approach often left patients weak and discour-
aged. In the 1950s new research concerning patient exercise tolerance
and cardiovascular function led to a different course of care. In the 1970s
Dr. Evans went about learning the theory, and implemented steps of this
new rehabilitative approach, and became the chief advisor to the Regional
Memorial Hospital Running Start program.

While the medical staff instituted changes in hospital care for heart
patients, Running Start developed a post-hospital cardiac rehabilitation
and a community adult fitness program. In 1978, Exercise Physiologist
Dee Merrill developed the operations for these programs, which provided
supervision and clinical monitoring by registered nurses, as patients and
community members went about reconditioning. Following a serious ill-

ness and the death of Ms. Merrill, the program has continued for over thirty years under the direction of Keith Guiou. The rehabilitation phase takes place in the hospital. The adult fitness program has operated at Brunswick Recreation Department, Coffin School and Bowdoin College's Sargent Gym, is now at the Farley Field House. Objectives are related to health needs of the community, reducing health costs, a working relationship with the community, using preventative medicine, and improving the quality of life. In 1996, a pulmonary rehabilitation program was added to support the needs of patients with chronic lung disease. Both cardiac and pulmonary rehabilitation programs have become certified by national organizations.

Regional took a leadership role in Cardiopulmonary Resuscitation (CPR) training with the formation of a program called 'Citizens for Cardiopulmonary Resuscitation (CCPR), Inc.' Regional nurses Patsy Cyr, Peg Johnson and Phyllis McGraves provided the necessary leadership on the project, including implementation of the American Heart Association standards for instructor training.

Early in the 1980s, a hospital committee—the Advocacy Committee for the Elderly (ACE)—addressed the growing needs of older persons in the community, proposing to the Regional administration the adoption of a "Lifeline" program: A volunteer, Marjorie Libby, together with Millie Stewart, Director of Volunteers, took the leadership roles. The Lifeline program provided a personal emergency response service designed to help provide security to area residents who were home bound, chronically ill, elderly, disabled and/or preferring to live alone. Over 500 Lifeline units are in the community today.

Peter Evans MD *and Celeste Pascarella* RN *early 1979 Running Start.*

Phyllis McGraves RN *and Gordon O'Donnell, long time Running Start participant.*

ADDICTION RESOURCE CENTER

In 1986 Bath opened a medical in-patient alcohol and drug detoxification program. Patricia Conner, a licensed alcohol and drug counselor, was hired to develop the program. The hospital opened a 10-bed unit named *One West* on August 20, 1986, with Dr. William Clark as medical director. Soon after, a community based program which had been providing a twenty eight day rehabilitation unit closed. Bath took on this program and further developed an intensive outpatient program for clients undergoing detoxification. Subsequently twelve beds were added for the rehabilitation program opening off campus in 1989 on Oak Grove Avenue. Beds previously assigned within the Bath hospital were transferred to the Oak Grove site.

Over the course of the next six to seven years, changes occurred in the treatment of addictions. New research showed that clients completing out-patient programs did just as well as those opting for inpatient care. Based on this new research, insurance companies began to deny authorization for the more costly inpatient programs, so the residential program closed in 1996. Outpatient programming eventually moved to 66 Baribeau Dr., Brunswick, providing individual, family and group counseling, intensive outpatient day and evening groups, and medication assisted treatment under the medical supervision of Dr. David Moltz.

THE FAMILY TREE

Another long-lasting health education effort initiated and sponsored by Regional Hospital is "The Family Tree." Coordinated by volunteer director Millie Stewart, this family wellness cable television program started in 1990 in partnership with Casco Cable TV and now for many years with Harpswell Community Television. Topics are determined by hospital and community representatives and "The Family Tree" host invites health care experts to discuss timely health issues. Program hosts over the years have included Sarah Hammond, Kathy McCatherine, Maureen Goudreau, Marla Davis RN, Marlise Swartz and now Cate Parker RN. Production has been accomplished for 24 years by camera women Harriet Paris and Millie Stewart. The program is broadcast by nine area cable stations, and continues to be an excellent channel of communication between Mid Coast Hospital and the communities it serves.

COMMUNITY HEALTH EDUCATION

Community health education became an important priority at Bath in the 1980s. Among the programs offered were babysitting, diabetes education, and childbirth education taught by maternity nurses.

"Womens' Wellness Day" was initiated at BMH and became a

Marla Davis RN *and Barbara Gordon* RN *opened Healthline, a community health information center sponsored by Mid Coast Hospital, at Cook's Corner Mall in 1995. The program offered health education, screenings and support groups. The program moved to the new hospital when it opened in 2001.*

popular annual spring event. The diabetes education program was initiated in the mid 1990s to support the needs of newly diagnosed diabetics to learn about the many aspects of their condition and to help prevent the vascular complications that can result. This comprehensive program included medication management, nutrition, the role of exercise and stress management. The program became by certified the American Diabetes Association and Dr. Daniel Wood served as medical advisor. In 2012 the diabetes education program moved to Mid Coast Hospital's newly developed Center for Diabetes and Endocrinology on the hospital campus.

In 1995 the new site of the hospital was still six years away. However, this did not prevent Mid Coast from developing a presence in the Cook's Corner neighborhood. The community health education program opened the aptly named storefront office, *Healthline,* at the Cook's Corner Mall on May 6, 1995 and brought together the health education activities of both Bath and Brunswick hospitals. Programs included outpatient wellness activities such as blood pressure clinics, diabetes education, nutrition consultation and tobacco cessation and was staffed by Marla Davis RN and Barbara Gordon RN. Services added later were children's safety, fall prevention clinics and evening programs on women's health issues. A Community Health Information Partnership (CHIP) initiated by Curtis Memorial Library and Parkview Adventist Medical Center provided yet another collaborative effort to support a

Mid Coast Hospital endorses fruit and vegetables in this 2007 photo. Adult carrot: Marla Davis RN, director for community health improvement, child carrot: Ian Fernald, potato: Victoria Chase, strawberry: Abby L'abbe, peapod: Delia Hickey.

healthy community. When the new Mid Coast Hospital opened in 2001, Healthline relocated to the main campus on Medical Center Drive.

Childbirth Education has always been a cornerstone of services for expectant parents. Over the years the program has adapted to the changes in maternity care; however, it has remained highly supportive of the entire childbirth experience. Program aspects include parent classes, lactation support, sibling preparation and Dad's Bootcamp.

COMMUNITY HEALTH IMPROVEMENT ENDOWMENT

Mid Coast Hospital's commitment to a strong community, a health and wellness program was emphasized once again in 2008 when, as part of the Certificate of Need application to enlarge the Medical/Surgical, Emergency and Diagnostic Imaging Departments, Robert McCue, chief financial officer, recommended starting a $3 million endowment dedicated to improving the health of the community. A major issue facing the Bath/Brunswick area, as well as the State of Maine and the nation, is childhood obesity. Marla Davis, the director for Community Health Improvement, was committed to addressing this problem. A program initiated by MaineHealth called the **5-2-1-0** was showing positive results in addressing this issue in York County, connecting the hospital to schools for the first time in an effort to increase fruit and vegetable consumption to **five** a day, decrease screen time to **two** hours per day, and increase physical activity to **one** hour per day, and limit sweetened drinks to **zero**. With the availability of the community health improvement, endowment funds became available to implement the program. The first year (2009) Davis worked with school champions/teachers, food services and students in Regional School Unit 1—Bath, West Bath, Woolwich, Phippsburg, and Georgetown. In the following three years the program was expanded to the Brunswick School Department, Maine School Administrative District #75, and several preschool programs and child-serving organizations in the region. The program emphasizes environmental and policy changes that are considered "best practice" approaches to improving weight and overall health of children.

ACCESS HEALTH: COMMUNITY HEALTH COALITION MODEL

In 1995, a fledgling community coalition consisting of Mid Coast at Bath and Brunswick, the American Cancer Society and the Bath and Brunswick Police Department began to collaborate on the troublesome issue of teen smoking. Called ACCESS Health (A Community Coalition Against Student Smoking), this group set out to inform the community about the problem and to inspire policy change to decease youth access to tobacco.

In 1999, Maine started receiving payments awarded by the Master Settlement Agreement (MSA), a lawsuit that required the four tobacco companies to pay for the harm caused by use of tobacco products and to change their marketing practices. The Fund for a Healthy Maine was established by the Maine Legislature to receive these funds and the Maine Centers for Disease Control & Prevention offered these and other federal grant funds to community coalitions prepared to address needs concerning tobacco control, physical activity and nutrition. ACCESS Health has successfully responded to Requests for Proposals from the Maine Center for Disease Control (CDC).

COMMUNITY MENTAL HEALTH

In January 1993 at the request of Herbert Paris, a group known as the Community Mental Health Committee, gathered to discuss the impact of the 1990 Maine Mental Health Consent Decree, court action setting out requirements to improve the mental health system in Maine. Community stakeholders invited to participate were Shoreline mental health provider, community services providers, law enforcement, consumers and advocates.

The first issue addressed related to police response to mental illness, resulting in the provision of an interdisciplinary training course for regional law enforcement, and enhanced communication between mental health providers and street-level law enforcement officers. The mental health committee was also instrumental in the 1994 adoption of a new state law which required "probable cause" prior to implementation of protective custody, and was endorsed by the Alliance for the Mentally Ill.

During the mid 1990s the committee fostered increased confidence, respect and communication among its members. Brunswick Deputy Police Chief Richard Mears was asked to lead a collaborative effort to rewrite the statewide training for police recruits in accordance with the model policy developed locally. In another innovative program, the members of the Shoreline Community Mental Health team began riding with police in Brunswick to improve their respective roles in supporting the mentally ill.

Over the last 20 years the group has continued to meet quarterly to strengthen interdisciplinary relationships and patient advocacy and to influence the integration of mental health services into primary care.

12

INTEGRATION *with the* TERTIARY CARE SERVICES *of* MAINE MEDICAL CENTER

WHILE THE MID COAST Health Services planning process was proceeding, a new organization related to our tertiary care provider, the Maine Medical Center, had developed and become known as MaineHealth. MaineHealth began to seek affiliations with a number of hospitals, developed primarily through a change of ownership of smaller community hospitals to become wholly owned subsidiaries of MaineHealth. These affiliates included not only Maine Medical Center, but Miles Hospital in Damariscotta, St. Andrews Hospital in Boothbay Harbor, Stevens Memorial Hospital in Norway, Penobscot Bay Medical Center in Rockland and other institutions. There was great pressure for Mid Coast Hospital to become an affiliate of MaineHealth, thus giving up its independence and becoming a wholly owned subsidiary. After lengthy discussions, there was no interest on the part of Mid Coast Hospital to move in this direction. However, it was important for Mid Coast to develop a strong clinical affiliation with Maine Medical Center. Following periods of intense discussion and cooling periods because of the resistance of Mid Coast, the process moved slowly until ultimately a strong affiliation agreement was developed between Maine Medical Center and Mid Coast Hospital. The medical center became the primary tertiary care institution working closely on a clinical basis with Mid Coast. This affiliation developed into a strong relationship with many

Mid Coast physicians taking leadership roles in the clinical directions of MaineHealth.

Mid Coast and its predecessors always had a strong clinical relationship with the Maine Medical Center, although there was no formal written document established. In 1994 a Memorandum of Understanding between Maine Medical and Mid Coast was signed providing for the opportunity to develop a shared vision for the proper provision of health care within the available resources. In fulfillment of these goals and further subject to applicable laws and public policies, which barred agreements in restraint of trade, a common understanding was reached for a more formal joint working relationship.

Each institution pledged that it would make their own administrative expertise available to the other. The expertise that existed in each organization would be shared with a goal of increasing the professionalism and skills available in each facility. It was further agreed that clinical expertise would be shared including nursing practices as well as other therapies and technologies. Also agreed was that the two institutions would work with their respective medical staff to inform physicians of the availability and scope of medical services available at their respective hospitals. As physicians independently determined appropriate referrals, patients might more readily receive an appropriate level of care in a site located close to home.

This Memorandum of Understanding recognized the autonomy of each hospital and is consistent with the goals of each. As this relationship matured, each hospital became more comfortable in working with its counterpart recognizing the significant difference in size, clinical expertise, and mission. A sense of mutual respect and admiration developed for what each contributed to the relationship. This ultimately lead to a more formal agreement between Mid Coast Health Services and MaineHealth in 1999, which further emphasized that the primary purpose of the relationship was to provide both organizations with an opportunity to work cooperatively and to improve quality in pursuing more effectively and efficiently their respective goals and visions of serving the healthcare needs of the communities.

Also understood was that Mid Coast Health Services and the organizations comprising MaineHealth would continue to compete in these activities in serving overlapping market areas and would continue to do so, except in those instances where an opportunity was identified and developed to improve quality and/or access with positive cost implications. This agreement was not intended to create any joint ventures or partnerships between the two institutions or change any corporate organization of each. A major goal of this agreement included efforts to effectively integrate community and tertiary hospital services, standardizing disease manage-

Scott Mills MD, *Vice President for Medical Affairs*

ment and other quality assurance efforts as well as collaborating in educational activities.

The clinical affiliation agreement between Mid Coast and Maine Medical continued to mature and a number of specialties began to develop protocols whereby patients needing the special resources of the tertiary care hospital would be transferred to Portland, together with the results of all tests and examinations done in Brunswick without repetition and then returned upon discharge, back to their primary care physicians or for rehabilitative services.

In 2007 Maine Medical Center developed an association with Tufts University School of Medical in response to a shortage of primary care physicians in Maine. They had been working together to develop a new medical school program designed to attract more Maine students into the field of medicine and thus train them in Maine with the hope and expectation that they would seek to practice within the state. Mid Coast was invited very early to engage with the Maine Medical Center/Tufts vision with the hope that they would be a participating community hospital in the training of medical students. Under the leadership of Dr. Scott Mills, Vice President for Medical Affairs for Mid Coast, this process was thoroughly investigated by a subcommittee of physicians and administration organized to examine the hospital's capacity and interest in being part of this new medical school as a clinical site. The hospital board of directors unanimously approved a recommendation that Mid Coast would become a clinical site for medical students in their junior year. Dr. Marybeth Ford, of the medical staff, was named the site's coordinator and worked closely with the Maine Medical Center/Tufts team to organize and develop the program.

13

CONTINUED GROWTH *of* MID COAST HOSPITAL

As we entered into the first decade of the new millennium Mid Coast Health Services experienced enormous growth. Hospital utilization rose, the emergency room began to fill up rapidly, stress between the Bath and Brunswick community eased, and Mid Coast increased its position as a major employer in the community. The Mid Coast Medical Group became a multi-specialty group practice with 70 employed physicians and 30 contracted physicians—hospitalists, pathologists, anesthesiologists, radiologists, psychiatrists and emergency room physicians. Efforts were significantly focused on improving the health status and well-being of the community with stronger emphasis on prevention and the role of the community health care organizations, such as Mid Coast, in providing universal access to the full array of prevention related services. Ties were strengthened with social service providers. Measuring system performance based upon outcomes became an important metric. Information for assessing Mid Coast Health Services' success in improving the health status of the community would become more accessible and powerful. This success would provide the fuel for continuous quality improvement efforts aimed at maximizing the value received for community health and social service investments and improving the vitality of the community they serve.

A major event in 2002 included the completion of a site master plan.

Through 2003 all services continued to grow—an expanded rehabilitation and physical therapy program was developed in a separate facility at 310 Bath Rd. with easy ground level access from the parking lot. A new digestive health center was created under the leadership of Dr. Alroy Chow with four new endoscopic suites. This freed up space in the main operating rooms and provided the gastroenterology physicians with space to provide services adjacent to their offices.

The capacity issue in the emergency room was addressed by adding treatment rooms and by managing flow and capacity. These changes became the key ingredient to seeing patients as quickly as possible.

A new information technology system was implemented with the capacity of interfacing hospital records electronically with physician's offices as well as home sites. Physicians have up to date data on their patients from both the emergency services as well as for special studies done in the laboratory, diagnostic imaging and pathology departments. A point of care computerized nursing documentation system moved us closer to a paperless record. Significant growth of the medical staff, particularly in the specialty areas, continued.

As pressures continued to mount on the available space in the new Mid Coast Hospital, and as the financial health of Parkview began to deteriorate, in 2004 senior management from both institutions held a series of meetings to explore whether or not the two organizations could come together.

While discussions were substantial and explored a variety of ways in which Parkview might become part of Mid Coast Health Services, the ideas were ultimately rejected by Parkview.

Since the opening in 2001, patient volume continued to grow at Mid Coast Hospital, with the hospital operating at or above its capacity. Because of the increasing utilization of its medical services, Mid Coast Hospital found it necessary to expand to meet the health care needs of the communities within its service area.

In the fall of 2006 an expansion plan was proposed and submitted to DHHS calling for a new and redesigned emergency department with additional treatment rooms, 18 additional beds to the medical/surgical inpatient unit; and additional space for the diagnostic imaging department. The project was budgeted at $22 million with no public fundraising drive—the funding would come from available hospital funds. Parkview again objected, but following public hearings the Certificate of Need was approved. The new wing opened in 2010. Mr. William Gardiner was the chairman of the hospital building committee and with great diligence provided oversight to the project.

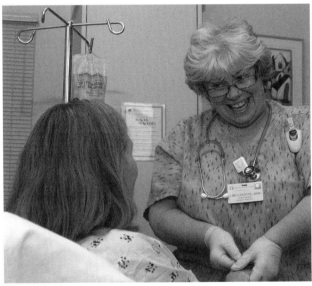

Lori Cooper RN

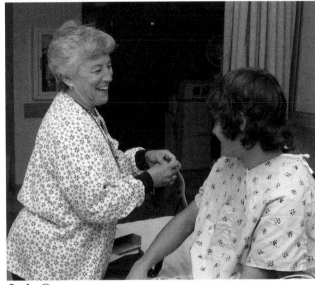

Judy Carver RN

During this period of time, Parkview's financial difficulties continued and in 2008 Central Maine Medical Center (CMMC) of Lewiston filed a Letter of Intent to acquire Parkview. CMMC had been providing physician coverage for Parkview's emergency room since the early 2000s. Within weeks of CMMC demanding payment for their services, Parkview signed an affiliation agreement with CMMC, subject to regulatory approvals. Additionally CMMC loaned Parkview $5.6 million, secured by a mortgage on Parkview's real estate. It included restricted covenants which, in effect, gave CMMC control of Parkview.

In December 2008, Mid Coast challenged CMMC's Certificate of Need to acquire Parkview on the grounds that it was unnecessary and duplicative. The community could no longer afford two hospitals. CMMC decided not to submit their C.O.N. at that time. For the next three years CMMC continued to operate Parkview through a management agreement. In 2012 CMMC again submitted a Letter of Intent to acquire Parkview. Mid Coast submitted a competing Certificate of Need to consolidate the health care services in the mid coast region. In 2013 CMMC withdrew their C.O.N. after informally receiving word that the C.O.N. staff was planning to deny their application and continued to operate Parkview through a management agreement. While Mid Coast repeatedly challenged the legality of this agreement, the state was reluctant to take action. Mid Coast remained hopeful that efforts would be ongoing that Parkview would find a way to sever this relationship with CMMC and work with Mid Coast to meet the health care needs of the community.

Progress at Mid Coast continued with the development of the new hospitalist program, a movement rapidly gaining popularity across the country including boards established in the specialty. Hospitalists provided full-time inpatient acute care coverage. Physicians and their office staffs continued to take care of their outpatient practices without the interruption of being called to the hospital for admitting their patients. Hospitalists are physicians of record while patients are in the hospital and take full control and responsibility for their care. They provide full reports to the primary care physicians for continuing care, following hospitalization.

14

CONCLUSION

T HE FINAL CHAPTER in the initial vision for the development of Mid
Coast Health Services was the completion of the Senior Health
Center. The Senior Health Center was a transformation of the Regional
Memorial Hospital and offered assisted living apartments, a memory im-
pairment unit, and rehabilitation and long term care beds, thus achieving
the full continuum of care throughout the Mid Coast system.

Today, the hospital has an active force of some 500 volunteers who
continue to support patient care services, raise funds for the hospital and
offer great enthusiasm and drive, which are translated into support from
the community.

The hospital was notified in May 2009, that it had received MAGNET
recognition by the American Nurses Credentialing Center, a branch of
the American Nurses Association. This notification was the culmina-
tion of over four years of incredible work by the staff under the leadership of Lois Skillings RN, Vice President for Nursing and Patient Care
Services and supported by staff members Paul Parker RN, Lauren Doran
RN, Deborah McLeod RN and Barbara McCue RN. MAGNET recognition
is an honor shared by less than 6% of hospitals in the United States and
indicates that the quality of care, working environment, and particularly
excellence of nursing care is of the highest caliber. Research shows that
patient outcomes are improved in MAGNET hospitals. Mid Coast Hospital

joined one other acute care hospital in Maine, the Maine Medical Center, in achieving MAGNET status. Mid Coast Hospital is the first and only community hospital in Maine to be awarded this recognition.

The MAGNET recognition project discovered from nursing research studies in the 1980s, that certain hospitals, even in the midst of nation-wide nurse shortages, had no difficulty attracting nurses, while many other hospitals could not find or retain nurses as easily. Certain administrative elements were consistent across all of these "MAGNET" facilities: primacy of the nurse/patient relationship, collaborative nurse/physician relationships, responsive and visionary nurse leadership, nursing staff control and autonomy over their clinical practices, and support by administration.

TRANSITIONS

In early 2010, Paris shared with the Board of Directors his desire to retire in the middle of 2011 and indicated that he would develop a transition plan. On January 1, 2010, Lois Skillings was appointed executive vice president. In the fall of 2010, Morrell, chair of the Mid Coast Health Services board, appointed a transition committee led by Ervin Snyder, vice chairman of the Mid Coast Hospital board, to evaluate the performance of Skillings in her role as executive vice president and her potential for leadership as the next president and chief executive officer.

To assess the performance of the executive vice president, a consultant was engaged and a broad ranging opinion survey was conducted with representatives of the senior management, medical staff, board members and selected department directors. Following that survey the transition committee had an in-depth interview with Skillings and formulated a recommendation. On February 24th, 2011, the board voted unanimously to appoint Skillings as the next president and chief executive officer of Mid Coast Health Services effective July 1, 2011 upon Paris's retirement.

REFLECTIONS

As staff prepared for transition into the second decade of the millennium the hospital embarked upon a comprehensive planning effort to develop a vision for the future of healthcare in the mid coast community and the role of Mid Coast Health Services in that vision. Skillings undertook that assignment which came to be known as the 2020 Vision, a road map for the future. The hospital had completed the 2000 vision established under the leadership of Paris.

The opening of the new hospital in 2001 was a monumental achievement that not only brought together the mid coast communities, but became a magnet to attract a top notch medical and hospital staff to the community. It was the "bricks and mortar" that allowed Mid Coast to be one of the most efficient, cost effective hospitals in Maine. Yet the work is never done. Skillings, as chair of the 2020 Vision project, began her work to create a vision so that Mid Coast Health Services would continue its leadership in transforming healthcare for the mid coast community. Priorities are:

- Continued prevention and wellness—an organization that not only takes care of patients when they become sick, but also takes responsibility for the health and well-being of our communities.

- Excellent patient experience—an organization that is easy to access and to navigate and is committed to delighting the customer. Caring is at the heart of what we do.

- Integrated accountable care—an organization that uses a team approach to manage quality and costs of healthcare across all settings, engaging the patient, the employers and the healthcare team in the process.

- Continuous improvement to achieve superior outcomes—an organization that continuously measures and improves everything we do and engineers safety, technology, and reliability into our clinical practice to achieve superior outcomes.

- Meeting community needs—an organization that actively engages with the community to plan for and meet changing needs and to provide a first place to turn for high quality health care close to home.

This vision, a composite involving hospital board directors, community members, patients, medical staff and hospital staff, has become the roadmap for the second decade of the millennium. In beginning the effort to implement aspects of the 2020 Vision, a new walk-in/primary care clinic was opened in downtown Brunswick at Maine Street Station in 2011 and provides easy access for quick care for minor health issues, as an alternative to the more expensive use of the emergency room.

MAGNET *ceremony 2009. Herbert Paris* CEO, *Lois Skillings* RN *and Paul Parker* RN

Barbara McCue RN

MAGNET *recognition at the state house. Deborah McLeod* RN, *Peggy Martin* RN, *Panee Coffin* RN, *Kathy Underwood* RN *and local State Legislators.*

Scott Mills MD *cuts the ribbon, opening the Primary Care and Walk-in Clinic at Brunswick Station*

15

EPILOGUE

Under lois skillings' leadership, Mid Coast continues to grow and flourish as the organization sets out to achieve its 2020 Vision. There are a number of significant initiatives that deserve further discussion.

BOARD REORGANIZATION

The change in executive leadership provided an opportune time to review Mid Coast's board structure. Over the preceding two decades the board structure had become very complex. With four separate boards overseeing each of the Mid Coast entities, board members and senior staff were spending significant time in board meetings. In 2013, a consultant was hired to develop options for a more streamlined board structure. After numerous meetings, what emerged was the concept of a "mirror" board whereby all board members would serve as the board of directors for all entities and could therefore conduct the business at one meeting per month rather than in four separate meetings. The recommendation from the consultant was unanimously approved by the Board in December 2013. Changes were made to the bylaws of each entity, and the Corporators approved the change in January 2014 at their annual meeting.

GROWTH OF THE MID COAST MEDICAL GROUP

Under the leadership of Dr. Mills, the Mid Coast Medical Group continues to grow by leaps and bounds and is fueling the growth of the entire health system. In the past three years, the medical group has added the specialties of Gastroenterology, Breast and Surgical Oncology, Rheumatology, Diabetes and Endocrinology, and General Surgery at Parkview. There are now nineteen Mid Coast Medical Group offices all sharing a common electronic health record. The success of the Primary Care and Walk-In Clinic in downtown Brunswick Station, opened in August 2011, has far exceeded expectations. Over 10,500 people used the Walk in Clinic in 2013. Often seen as an alternative to the Emergency Department for people with minor injuries or illness, the Walk-In Clinic helps to improve access to healthcare while lowering the cost of care. The clinic also supports Bowdoin College Health Services by providing easy access to care for students after hours and on weekends.

NEW MEDICAL OFFICE BUILDINGS IN TOPSHAM AND BATH

In 2014, the Topsham Internal Medicine practice opened its new offices on the campus of the Highlands on the Coastal Connector in Topsham. This building is one of the first in Maine to incorporate the concepts of the "Patient Centered Medical Home" which includes much more emphasis on team space for the physician and other members of the care team such as social workers and nurse care coordinators. The building included "shell" space for future growth. The demand for Mid Coast primary care has grown so quickly that plans are already underway to complete the shell space and add physicians and nurse practitioners.

A similar evolution of the Bath Internal Medicine practice has begun in Bath. Construction has begun on a 20,000 square foot medical office building on Centre Street in downtown Bath that will also be based on the new "Patient Center Medical Home" design concepts. Occupancy will take place in the spring of 2015.

CONTINUED COMMITMENT TO QUALITY

Mid Coast Hospital continues to be in the top tier of quality scores for community hospitals in Maine. The dedication to excellence in patient care and services remains a top priority. Mid Coast Hospital achieved Commission on Cancer Accreditation in 2012, becoming one of only ten hospitals in Maine to hold this designation. In 2012, Mid Coast Hospital became the fourth hospital in the State of Maine to become accredited as a Primary Certified Stroke Center by the Joint Commission. In 2014, the American Nurses Credentialing Center re-designated Mid Coast as a Magnet hospital; one of only two Magnet hospitals in Maine. In the United States, only 25 hospitals under 100 beds have achieved Magnet designation.

In January 2014, a major phase of the Affordable Care Act went into effect whereby all Americans were required by law to have health insurance. Access to health insurance was accomplished by providing tax credits to persons with incomes between 138% and 400% of the poverty limit and expanding Medicaid for persons with incomes between 100% and 138% of the poverty limit. To date, Maine has chosen not to expand Medicaid so that the percentage of Mainers without health insurance has not changed significantly.

Other aspects of the Affordable Care Act are impacting Mid Coast more directly. The Act creates incentives for healthcare organizations to be more accountable for the total cost and the quality of the care that they provide. For example, there are now payment penalties for hospitals that have higher than average re-admission rates. Mid Coast has an entire team and infrastructure dedicated to the "accountable care" activities.

Since 2012, declining reimbursement to hospitals due to planned Medicare cuts and the sluggish economy, combined with growing large deductible payments in the private sector, has created a perfect storm for financial challenges to hospitals today. At Mid Coast, the free care and bad debt portion of the budget has doubled in the last five years to total nearly $13 million in 2014. At the same time, inpatient utilization rates continue to decrease all over the country in great part due to efforts to improve ambulatory services and chronic illness management. In spite of these challenges, Mid Coast Hospital remains in a positive financial position and is considered one of the most cost effective community hospitals in Maine, with costs twenty-five percent below the state average.

As of this writing, efforts continue with Parkview Adventist Medical Center to open a discussion toward a vision of bringing the two organizations together in a manner that will allow our communities to continue to have high quality and affordable healthcare for decades to come.

This changing landscape of national health reform, along with exponential and transformative changes in healthcare delivery and technology, will shape the next decade in ways we cannot begin to imagine today.

APPENDIX — I
COMMUNITY HEALTH AND NURSING SERVICES

Years	Location	Leadership	Comments
1931–49	72 Front Street, Bath City Directories	Ruth Weeks Henry, RN	1947: Transition from RC Nursing to PH Nursing Association
1949–50	71 Front Street		
1955–56, 59–62	72 Front Street	RWH retired 1956	
1963–64	55 Front Street		
1965–66		Bernice Brawn RN	
1967–77	Bath Memorial Hospital	Doris Watson RN DON 1973: Robert Liversage ED	1973: Bath Brunswick Regional Health Agency/Bath Visiting Nurses had PT offices also at RMH and Parkview
1976–78	4 Park Street, Bath	Doris Watson	1978: Became Community Health & Nursing Services
1978–82	Gulf Station, Vine St.		Gulf Station demolished in 1983
1982–87	Hennessey Ave.	Laura Cathcart ED	
1987–2005	50 Baribeau Drive, Brunswick	Jean St. Amand, ED, Stormy Ellis, Julie L'Heureux, ED	1993 Acquired by Mid Coast Health Services
2005	60 Baribeau Drive	Darlene Chalmers ED	
2010			Merger of Hospice Volunteers into CHANS

APPENDIX - 2
HOSPITAL AUXILIARY PRESIDENTS

BATH MEMORIAL AUXILIARY

1944–48	Marion King
1948–50	Eleanor Voorhees
1950–52	Virginia Gilles
1952–54	Marion Dean Shaw
1954–56	Ellena Sewall
1956–57	Katherine Torrey
1958	Ruth Francisco
1959–60	Diane Henderson Francis
1961–62	Molly Luke
1963–65	Henrietta Mayo
1966–68	Julia Whitehurst
1967–68	Sylvia Katz
1969–70	Muriel "Susie" Marsh
1971–72	Jean W. Grant
1972–74	Esther Dougherty
1975–76	Thyra R. Levin
1977–78	Beverly Emero
1979–81	Elizabeth Akar
1981–82	Jody Simpson
1982–84	Roberta Doyle
1984–86	Carol Mulligan
1986–86	Gail Buck
1986–88	Jane Chapin
1988–90	Marguerite Small
1990–92	Dorothy Kelly
1992–94	Dorothy Shorette
1994–96	Shirley Richelieu
1996–2001	Beryl R. McPherson

BRUNSWICK COMMUNITY HOSPITAL AUXILIARY

1956–58	Mabel Matthews
1958–60	Louise Abelon

REGIONAL MEMORIAL HOSPITAL AUXILIARY

12/60–11/62	Charlotte Rose
11/62–11/64	Martha Coles
11/64–66	Lucy Shulman
1966–68	Catherine T. Daggett
1968–70	Gertrude Ring
1970–72	Martha "Haffy" Gould
1972–74	June Marden
1974–76	Jean VanDeventer
1976–78	Helen Freeman
1978–80	Marion Weber
1980–82	Martha Greenlaw
1982–84	Eileen Cole
1985–86	Audrey Parkinson
1987–88	Deborah Gleason
1989–90	Margit Cook
1992–94	Lois Berge
1994–96	Executive Committee
1997–2000	Margi Sumner
2000–01	Eleanor Patterson

MID COAST HOSPITAL AUXILIARY

2001–02	Eleanor Patterson
2002–04	Beverly Wilson
2004–06	Abigail Manny
2006–08	Nancy Schlieper
2008–10	Eleanor Tracy
2010–11	Abigail Manny
2011–13	Carolyn Gibson
2013–15	Ellen Hutchinson

APPENDIX 3
HOSPITAL BOARD CHAIRS

Hon. John S. Hyde

BCH   1907–1917

Hon. Charles W. Clifford

BCH   1917–1918

Hon. William D. Sewall

BCH   1918–1928

Henry C. Wright

BCH   1928–1933

L. Eugene Thebeau

BMH   1933–1937

Hon. Arthur Sewall

BMH   1937–1945

Hon. Donald N. Small

BMH   1945–1946

W. Dayton Hill

BMH   1946–1947

Archibald M. Main

BMH   1947–1961

Avery M. Fides

RMH   1957–1964

Raymond C. Small

BMH   1961–1966

Emerson W. Zeitler

RMH   1964–1969

Duncan McInnes

BMH   1966–1970

Sanford B. Cousins

RMH   1969–1971

George Baer Connard

BMH   1970–1981

Harry G. Shulman

RMH   1971–1974

Mrs. F. Webster Browne

RMH   1974–1977

Charles R. Rooney

RMH   1977–1979

Richard A. Morrell

RMH   1979–1984, '87–'88

MCHS   1991–2012

Leonard C. Mulligan

BMH   1981–1985

Edward F. Wilson

RMH   1984–1987

Janet B. Bussey

BMH   1985–1989

Campbell B. Niven

RMH   1988–1990

Nicholas S. Sewall

BMH   1989–1991

Frank Goodwin

RMH   1990–1991

David R. Flaherty

MCH   1992–1993

Stephen C. Harris

MCH   1994–1995

John Moncure

MCH   1996–1998

William F. King, JR.

MCH   1999–2001

Charles F. Richelieu

MCH   2002–2004

Mary Lou Kennedy

MCH   2005–2006

John G. Morse, IV

BMH   2007–2009
MCHS   2012–2014

Charles D. Frizzle

MCH   2010–2011

Ervin D. Snyder

MCH   2012–2013

Barbara Reinertsen

MCHS   2014

APPENDIX 4
ADMINISTRATORS

BATH CITY HOSPITAL

1909-1911	Carrie E. Goodwin, RN
1911–1912	C. L. Butterfield, RN
1912–1919	Charlotte Marshall, RN
1919	Ella A. Derrick, RN
1919–1920	E. A. Gillett, RN
1920	Jennie F. Stannix, RN
1920–1925	Margaret F. Robert, RN
1925–1927	M. E. Furbish, RN
1927–1933	Helen Downing, RN

BATH MEMORIAL HOSPITAL

1934–1941	Helen Downing
1941–1945	Gladys Wolstenholme, RN
1945–1946	Yellena Seevers, RN
1947–1955	Miss Downing, RN
1955–1956	Thelma B. Ward, RN
1956–1973	Katherine Ames, RN
1974–1985	David Kelly
1985–1987	J. Neil Bassett

REGIONAL MEMORIAL HOSPITAL

1960–1971	Louis Dye
1971–1974	Jeffrey White
1974–1977	Robert Petit
1978–1987	Herbert Paris

MID COAST HEALTH SERVICES/MID COAST HOSPITAL

1987–2011	Herbert Paris
2011–	Lois Skillings, RN

REFERENCES:

1. William Purington, *Look into West Bath's Past*, 1976, pg. 119

2. Wheeler and Wheeler, *History of Brunswick and Topsham*, pg. 214

3. Parker M. Reed, *History of Bath*, 1895

4. Henry W. Owens, Edward Clarence Plummer, *History of Bath*, 1936

5. Discover Maine, Volume 10, Issue 7, 2013, *Western Lakes and Mountain Region*, Page 75

6. The Lewiston Journal, June 12, 1927

7. George O. Cummings MD, *Maine General Hospital, An Historical Sketch*, The Journal of Maine Medical Association, August 1960

8. Hatch. *The History of Bowdoin College*, pg. 466

9. Abraham Flexner, *Medical Education in the United States and Canada (New York: The Carnegie Foundation for the Advancement of Teaching 1910)*

10. Charles Calhoun, *A Small College in Maine, 200 Years at Bowdoin*, pg. 116

11. Maine Medical Association Sesquicentennial Celebration Program, November 8, 2003, Page 7–8

12. Owen, *History of Bath, Ibid*, pg. 316–17

13. Christine H. Curtis, *The Bath Hospital Training School for Nurses*, Unpublished Manuscript 2000

14. P.L. Pert. *1918 Flu Epidemic Struck Bath Three times*, The Times Record, January 9, 1989.

15. Bath Memorial Hospital Board of Trustee Minutes 1943–1944

16. Kenneth R. Martin and Ralph Linwood Snow, *The Maine Odyssey 1936-86*, pg. 117–118

17. Bath Memorial Hospital Board of Trustee Minutes 1944

18. Bath Daily Times, January 20, 1945

19. Bath Memorial Hospital Board of Trustee Minutes April 11, 1945

20. Bath Daily Times, April 2, 1945

21. Bath Memorial Hospital Board of Trustee Minutes 1945–1946

22. Bath Memorial Hospital Board of Trustee Minutes 1959–1960

23. Interview with Margaret Dunlop and Helen Johnson

24. Annette Vance Dorey, Harpswell, ME. Based on interviews with Mrs. Dorothy Hall, RN, Marjorie Libby, Brunswick, ME, Juliet Messier, Brunswick, ME

25. Brunswick Record, Vol. 35, No. 48, October 2, 1937, Page 3

26. Minutes of Organizing Committee for Regional Memorial Hospital 1957

27. University of Vermont College of Medicine, *The Brunswick Area—A Study on Hospital Needs, November 1957, Funded by The Commonwealth Fund*, Page 60–68

28. The Brunswick Times, November 28, 1957

29. Regional Memorial Hospital Board of Director Minutes, March 13, 1957

30. Correspondence and document between Dr. Bettle and Dr. Weaver, October 17, 1956

31. Living history discussion between Herbert Paris and Mrs. F. Webster Browne, past chairperson of Board of Trustees and one of original founding trustees of Regional Memorial Hospital, December 30, 2000.

32. Brunswick Times, March 27, 1974

33. Marla Davis. *Ruth Weeks Henry, RN: The Remarkable Life of a 20th Century Nurse*, Bath Historical Society Newsletter Number 97, Jan–March 2008.

34. Ernst and Young Feasibility Study to build a new hospital, 1998

35. Florence Nightingale, *Notes on Nursing*, Page 33, 1974

TIMELINE

1982   RMH New ORs/ER/Front Entrance

1985   Bath Brunswick Shared Services Corp./CT Scan

1986   Consolidation of Administration, Finance, Planning Fund Raising with Bath Memorial Hospital

1991   Merger—Formation of Mid Coast Health Services/Mid Coast Hospital

1986   Planning/consolidation of Regional Memorial Hospital/Bath Memorial Hospital

1987   Special joint meeting of Corporators to approve consolidation for administration/fundraising/planning fundraising

1987   Plans developed for Thornton Oaks

1987   Mere Point Nursing Home purchase

1989   Regional Memorial Hospital/Bath Memorial Hospital purchase of Cook's Corner land

       Mid Coast Hospital named

1992   Temporary building to house Cardiology

1992   CON submitted for new hospital

1993   Community Health and Nursing Services (CHANS) acquired

1993   Mid Coast Medical Group organized

1996   Mid Coast Health Services announce plans to close Bath Memorial Hospital inpatient and convert ER to Urgent Care

1997   Parkview withdraws challenge and court decisions vacated

1997   New architect selection and modification of plans

1997   Bath Hospital inpatient vacated

1998   Construction begins

2001   New hospital opens

2002   Conversion of Regional Memorial Hospital to Senior Health Center

2002   Bath Memorial Hospital sold to City of Bath for $1.00 for conversion to Community College

2010   Addition to Mid Coast Hospital opens

2010   Hospice merges into CHANS

2011   Paris retires—Skillings named CEO

2011   Walk-in clinic opens

BIBLIOGRAPHY

Ralph Linwood Snow, *Bath Iron Works—The First Hundred Years* (Anthoensen Press, Portland, Maine—John G. Morse, Jr.—Publisher, 1987)

Kenneth R. Martin and Ralph Linwood Snow, *Maine Odyssey—Good Times and Hard Times in Bath, 1936-1986,* (Patten Free Library, Bath, Maine, 1988)

Lincoln P. Paine, *Down East—A Maritime History of Maine,* (Tilbury House, Gardiner, Maine, 2000)

Sesquicentennial of Bath, Maine, 1847-1997, (Bath Historical Society, 1997)

Bill Caldwell, *Rivers of Fortune,* (Gannett Press, Portland, Maine, 1983

Henry Wilson Owen, *History of Bath, Maine,* (The Times Company, Bath, Maine, 1936)

George A. Wheeler and Henry W. Wheeler, *History of Brunswick, Topsham and Harpswell, Maine,* (New Hampshire Publishing Company in collaboration with the Pejepscot Historical Society, 1974)

Lewis C. Hatch, *History of Bowdoin College,* (Loring, Short and Harmon, Portland, Maine, 1927)

Paul Starr, *The Social Transformation of American Medicine,* (Basic Books, A Division of Harper Collins, 1982)

Joyce K. Bibber, *Images of Bath and West Bath,* (Arcadia Publishing 1995)

William Avery Baker, *A Maritime History of Bath, Maine and The Kennebec River Region,* (Marine Research Society of Bath, Volumes 1 and 2, 1973)

Neil Rolde, *Maine Downeast and Different,* (American Historical Press, 2006)

Maine History, Volume 46, #1, (Maine Historical Society, October 2011)